Sheffield Wednesday

Illustrating the Greats

Published & Printed by Pickard Communication,
10-11 Riverside Park, Sheaf Gardens, Sheffield S2 4BB
Telephone 0114 275 7222 or 275 7444
Facsimile 0114 275 8866
email info@picomm.co.uk
www.picomm.co.uk

Introduction

I first saw Sheffield Wednesday at Hillsborough when I was 5 years old in April 1955. It was a glorious 5-0 hammering of WBA, the last match of the season but sadly Wednesday were relegated to Division Two. The next season was brilliant, I was still being informed who all the players were, but we kept winning and the noise from the crowd as the goals were scored was intoxicating. All five of the Wednesday forward line scored into double figures and the Owls were promoted as champions. The next few seasons were more of the same, another relegation and another Division Two Championship. I was hooked.

Then came the glorious early sixties: three years under manager Harry Catterick, second spot in Division One behind the double winning Spurs side and an FA Cup semi-final against Blackburn Rovers. Plus there were international players like Springett, Swan, Kay and Fantham displaying their talents for the Owls. This, sadly, was followed by the shattering bribes scandal, which involved the aforementioned Swan, Kay and also our top scorer David Layne. In 1966 the moral sapping FA cup final defeat against Everton did nothing to help and Wednesday began a slide that within four years would lead them into division two. We had bounced back before, not to worry.

The seventies started with relegation and can only be said to have been a depressing decade for any Sheffield Wednesday fan. I recall attending Hillsborough in April 1975 against Norwich City in a crowd of less than seven and a half thousand people, one of the smallest crowds I have ever seen, and witnessed the Owls defeated 0-1. In Wednesday's last 17 games of the 1974-75 season they only managed to score twice and gain one point. The top scorer was Eric McMordie, who played in 9 games and scored 6 goals. Relegation was assured. Division three was a stressful few years but by the end of the decade, the Owls seemed on the up.

The resurgence in the eighties was glorious to see. We had a side that played some fine football, players who could score 20 plus goals in a season and a high position of fifth in the top flight and two FA cup semi finals.

It was the big time in the nineties with innumerable visits to Wembley: League Cup winners, against Manchester United (that was sweet), League Cup runners-up and semi-finalists and FA cup runners up after a replay against Arsenal. There was the famous Wembley semi-final victory against the old enemy from across the city, Sheffield United and we finished third in the top division and qualified for Europe (a feat not achieved for about 30 years).

More recently, after going through another two relegation seasons we found ourselves in the ludicrously titled League One (which to you and me means Division Three). Times have been leaner but the fans, in large numbers, still keep visiting Hillsborough in anticipation of what can, and hopefully, will be.

So it is from this 50 year rollercoaster ride of visiting Hillsborough and seeing the ups and down of the Owls, I decided I would like to pick out the players who have given me most pleasure whilst watching Sheffield Wednesday. Some of them, I know, you will wholeheartedly agree with. Some of them will cause a possible "he would never have got in my top list of players", and unless you are as old as me some of them you may not even have heard of.

Gary Mackender has illustrated all the players for the book and as you will see he is an extremely talented artist. He has the qualification for this job not only because he is a graphic and commercial artist but also a Sheffield Wednesday season ticket holder and has been for a number of years. Gary is a true Wednesdayite.

Abby Currier, a family friend, has illustrated the selection of five managers. At only 15 years of age she is an exceptionally talented artist with a very bright future. She is also an Owl.

I hope this book "Illustrating the Greats" will bring back some happy memories.

Contents

Contents *continued*

Sheffield Wednesday

Illustrating the Greats

Ronnie **Starling**

Having never seen this pre-war Sheffield Wednesday inside forward play you may ask how he comes to be included in the list of my personal all time greats.

My grandfather Charles Richard Otley was a huge fan of Ronnie Starling and even named his only son, my uncle Ronald James Ernest Otley, after him. My uncle was born in 1938 just three years after Sheffield Wednesday had won the English Football Association Cup Final in 1935. My grandfather lost a brother, James, sadly killed in the Battle of the Somme in the First World War, but his name still came second after his beloved "Ronnie". So as you can imagine, when growing up I heard plenty about Starling from my grandfather. "Full of guile that Starling" is the way he used to describe his favourite player.

He is the only Sheffield Wednesday player I have ever seen a picture of carrying the much vaunted FA Cup.

Ronnie Starling was born in 1909 and at the age of 14 started work down the pit. He worked at two north-east collieries, Unsworth and Washington respectively, before he was spotted playing amateur football by Hull City Manager, Bill McCracken who promptly signed him.

He was at Hull City for three years, all spent in the second division. In season 1929-30 Hull City were playing some glorious football and managed to reach the semi-final of the FA Cup. They even managed to take the mighty Arsenal to a replay before defeat stopped them one win short of a cup final appearance.

Soon after the semi-final, Starling was transferred to Newcastle United for £4,000,

Ronnie Starling (Sheff Wed & England)

but was never really taken to by the Geordie fans. He missed out on being selected for the Newcastle FA Cup winning side of 1932 and shortly afterwards, during the summer, he was transferred to Wednesday.

At the beginning of 1932-1933 season, he began his five year stay at Sheffield Wednesday. His career, which had stalled at Newcastle, was back on track. He was signed by Robert Brown, but within a season there was a new man in charge of the Owls, Billy Walker. It was Walker who figured you had to cajole Starling to extract the best football from him. He made him captain and the central figure in midfield. Ronnie responded to this and played some of the best football of his career, culminating in the 1935 Cup Final win against West Bromwich Albion 4-2. Starling controlled midfield and sprayed some glorious passed to the Wednesday forwards.

Ronnie played for Wednesday for another couple of years, until January 1937, when he moved on to Aston Villa. He made an immediate impact playing in Villa's promotion winning side in 1938. The same season they also reached the FA Cup final. He remained at Villa Park all through the war years and did not retire until 1948 when aged 39. After his retirement he was, for a time, coach at Nottingham Forest.

He played 178 league and 17 FA cup games for Sheffield Wednesday, scoring 31 goals all in the league. His goalscoring was never prolific. Eight goals in seasons 1932-33 and 1933-34 were his highest returns. He played with Wednesday for just over four years.

He won only one full England cap, this was against Scotland in 1933. Sheffield Wednesday, unfortunately, seem to have a number of players, 13 to be precise, who have only managed one cap, John Fantham, Gerry Young and Mel Sterland amongst them.

Ronnie Starling, sadly, passed away on 17th December 1991 at the age of 82.

Wednesday

Jackie **Robinson**

Jackie Robinson (Sheff Wed & England)

The reason this player is included in my list is similar to Ronnie Starling, but this time the admirer is my father, who is a dyed in the wool unitedite. He still says that Robinson was the best inside forward he has ever seen, this includes his beloved Jimmy Hagan.

Jackie Robinson was born in Shiremoor, in the North East, near Sunderland on 10th August 1917 he played for his county when only 13 years of age and was destined to be a star for whichever team were lucky enough to gain his services. Thankfully that team was Sheffield Wednesday.

Jackie Robinson's first game for the Owls, at the age of 17, was at the end of season 1934-1935, on 22nd April, Easter Monday, against West Bromwich Albion, he scored in a 1-1 draw. Weeks later Wednesday played West Brom again and beat them 4-2 in the FA Cup Final. Jackie had not yet established himself in the team and was just taken along to Wembley as a non playing member of the Sheffield Wednesday Party.

The next season, 1935-36 Jackie played five games but did not score. 1936-37 proved to be a different prospect he played 29 league games scored 6 goals and showed enough class to be selected for England. Not bad for a 19 year old. The year after, 1938, he was selected for England another three times. The game against Germany in 1938, when the English players were pressured by the British government to give the Nazi salute, was Jackie's international highlight, a 6-3 win and he scored two of the goals himself.

Unfortunately for Jackie, the Second World War robbed him of displaying his talents as often as he should have been allowed and six years out of his career was lost whilst Europe was in conflict. Jackie still managed to play over 100 games for

the Wednesday in the the war years, score 90 goals and made a war time Cup Final (Northern) appearance for Sheffield Wednesday against Blackpool in 1942-1943 in a two legged tie. Unfortunately for the Owls a loss and a draw, 1-2 at Hillsborough and 2-2 at Blackpool saw the cup go to Lancashire. As usual Jackie scored a goal in both games. The attendance at the Hillsborough game was a wartime record 47,657 (receipts of £5,965). In the 1942-43 season Jackie knocked in 6 hat trick.

In the four years before the war Jackie scored 38 goals in 110 games. He scored 90 goals in 100 wartime appearances. After the war in season 46-47 Jackie only played 6 games for Wednesday scoring 6 goals before he was transferred back to his roots, Sunderland.

Jackie played with Raich Carter and an up and coming young star called Len Shackleton at Sunderland, what a forward line. He only played two full seasons with Sunderland but in his 85 games still managed to score 34 times, a good return from any forward.

The now ageing Robinson was offered a coaching post at Lincoln City, an offer too good to turn down for a footballer in his 32nd year. Unfortunately after only a handful of games he was injured, whilst in the process of scoring, and this injury put an end to his playing career.

Jackie, who sadly passed away in 1972, will be remembered as one of the all time Sheffield Wednesday greats

My father said that Jackie played a little better with a couple of pints inside him - a story I have seen in print and heard from other sources.

In his early days with Wednesday he lodged with Robert and Jessie Wrigley on Dorothy Road in Hillsborough.

Just to prove that the man still has appeal for the Sheffield public a new book entitled "The Jackie Robinson Story" has been produced by Eric Brodie and Alan Triolett which gives a good insight into club and international football in a much more gentlemanly era.

Wednesday

Redfern **Froggatt**

Redfern Froggatt was signed from Sheffield YMCA in 1943 and played in 86 wartime games for Wednesday before his FA cup debut in 1946 and his League debut in the opening game of 1946-47 season.

Redfern Froggatt was born in Sheffield on August 23rd 1924. Twenty one and a half years later, on January 5th 1946, he made his debut proper for Sheffield Wednesday in a FA Cup tie. In that first season with the first team he only played six games, all in the FA Cup. Even in those early games his goalscoring prowess showed through. He scored three goals in those six appearances.

From season 1946-47 and for the following 14 seasons, Froggatt was almost a permanent first team fixture. He was also unusual in that he played well into his mid thirties, when most players of that era were retiring at around 30 and taking up a local pub or club occupancy.

In fact in his 34th year Redfern played some of his best football and showed his best goal-scoring return, in 38 games he notched 26 goals. Froggatt scored into double figures on eight out of his fourteen seasons with Wednesday. Wednesday were relegated and promoted four times in the fifties. Redfern actually won three Second Division Championship Medals

Redfern Froggatt (Sheff Wed & England)

A one club man, his career spanned over 16 years with Sheffield Wednesday. You don't get too many players who stay that long at any club nowadays. This is possibly because the agents whom the players all seem to employ, don't make money if their client stay with one club for too many years. Transfers are where the profit are made.

Froggatt played in 433 league games and scored 140 league goals. He also appeared in 24 FA Cup ties and scored nine goals. This does not include any of his wartime appearances or goals. Counting all his appearances, he played well over 500 games and possibly scored more than 170 goals for Wednesday. His final appearance for Sheffield Wednesday was in the last game of the 1959-1960 season.

His 140 league goals became the highest number of post war goals scored by any Wednesday player. Unfortunately, Redfern only held that record for eight years, until a young chap he played alongside, in the last three years of his Hillsborough career, Johnny Fantham surpassed it by a further 7 goals. Fantham amassed a career total of 147 league goals, which will probably stand forever.

Redfern Froggatt was selected for Full England international duty on four occasions. His first cap was against Wales in 1952. In 1953 against Scotland he played in a left wing partnership with his cousin Jack Froggatt who was with Portsmouth FC. The fact that Froggatt also played over 50 games for Wednesday on the left wing makes his goalscoring record look even better.

Froggatt was not only noted for his goalscoring ability but also for his skill at making chances for others. When you consider who he played with in his time with Wednesday and the goals these players scored it really does show how classy a player he was. Derek Dooley 1951-1952 season, 30 games, 46 goals, Eddie Quigley only 78 games in total for Wednesday but returned a very respectable 52 goals, Jackie Sewell 156 games - 81 goals, Roy Shiner 160 games - 96 goals, Albert Quixall in 1956-57 season, 42 games 24 goals and finally John Fantham who was to go on and break Redfern's post war scoring record.

Redfern sadly passed away in December 2003 aged 79.

Wednesday

Derek **Dooley**

Derek Dooley a young man from the Pitsmoor/Firth Park area of Sheffield, signed for Wednesday in 1947 after a brief spell as an amateur at Lincoln City. I suppose by today's standards Derek had a tough time as a youngster with the

Derek Dooley (Sheffield Wednesday)

Owls. He scored prolifically in the Yorkshire League and Central League (Sheffield Wednesday Reserves) and was given his chance in 1949-1950 season. He was given one game but didn't score, and by all accounts he looked a little out of place. There were no more chances that season. 1950-1951, again one game and no score, and once again not a great display. No more chances that season either

In October 1951, Derek was given his third first team outing. This time he took his chance with aplomb, two goals scored and a bustling display. Derek must have thought 'drop me now'! Just to make sure they didn't drop him he banged in another 18 goals in his next 10 games. Derek Dooley had arrived at Hillsborough, albeit four years after he first signed up for them.

In that 1951-1952 season Derek knocked in five goals against Notts County, four goals against Everton and Hull City and three goals against West Ham United and Brentford. He eventually finished the season with 46 league goals from 30 league games and a goal in the one FA Cup match he played, to give final figures of 47 goals from 31 games.

The crowd's response to Dooley's goals was amazing, they took him to their hearts and manipulated a hit of the day, a Guy Mitchell Song, 'Truly Truly Fair', to, yes you've guessed: 'Dooley Dooley's there'. Here was one of our own banging goals in for fun, and looking as though no defender could stop him.

Wednesday won promotion that season and great things were expected for 1952-53.

Alas, Derek Dooley and Sheffield Wednesday both found life a little harder than expected in the First Division. Goals didn't come anywhere near as frequently as they had been coming the year before in the lower division and Wednesday struggled for nearly all of the season. Dooley, after a poor start seemed to find the goalscoring touch again and started to score on average more than a goal every 2 games, not quite his Second Division ratio but still very respectable. His season tally showed 29 games played, 16 goals scored. He was joint top scorer with Jackie Sewell. Unfortunately, on St Valentine's Day, 14th February 1953 Derek broke his leg in a challenge with the Preston North End goalkeeper at Deepdale. Derek was taken to a Preston hospital where his leg was placed in plaster. Derek with his jovial attitude asked a nurse to sign his plaster cast. While doing so the nurse noticed that Derek did not feel her touch his foot. The plaster was quickly removed and it was discovered that gangrene had infected his leg. The only option to save Derek's life was amputation. At 23 years of age Derek Dooley had played his final game for Sheffield Wednesday.

Derek was to become Development Fund Organiser in 1962 and was still in this position when Danny Williams, the manager was sacked. Derek was offered the job, which he quickly accepted in February 1971. 1972-73 started very well and Wednesday even topped the division two table for a while. The Owls faded away and finished only 10th. In season 1973-74, Derek did not have the best of luck with injuries, in fact a virus that spread through the club and affected 16 players plus Derek himself caused two months of mayhem when untried youngsters and unfit regulars were sent out to represent the Owls. On Christmas Eve 1973 Derek Dooley was sacked. Even by today's standards in football that had to be deemed heartless, especially to a man who was Wednesday through and through. Derek cut his ties with Wednesday and not until 21 years later, 1994, did he set foot in the Hillsborough ground.

He moved on to Sheffield United where he became commercial manager, then director, and managing director.

At all levels, Yorkshire League, Central League, Football League, Derek Dooley scored 180 goals in 168 matches for Sheffield Wednesday. Not too bad a record.

Wednesday

Albert **Quixall**

Quixall was destined to make the big time at one sport or another. He played football, cricket, tennis, badminton and table tennis all to a very high standard. But whilst at Meynell Road school he was capped for England Schoolboys at soccer and was on the path to a very successful career that was to carry on for nearly another two decades. He made a promise to his father that he wouldn't go to any club but Sheffield Wednesday. His father, who was a greenkeeper at Firth Park, was made a happy man when Wednesday took Albert on to their groundstaff straight from school.

Quixall worked his way through the ranks very quickly: Yorkshire League, Central League, and in February 1951, his football league debut against Chelsea. Making his debut on the same day was another young man Alan Finney, who was three months Albert's junior. They were close friends and became almost permanent fixtures in the Wednesday side for seven years before Albert was sold. In fact Alan Finney stayed with Sheffield Wednesday until the cup final season of 1966. I am led to believe they were nicknamed 'Null and Void' by the rest of their team mates. I cannot find or proffer an explanation for these nicknames.

Over the following seven and a half seasons Albert became "The Golden Boy" of Sheffield football. He scored 64 goals in 241 league appearances, slightly better than a one in four ratio. This from a midfielder who played just behind the strikers is no mean feat. Albert really did look the part, easily recognisable with his big quiff of blonde hair, quick feet and a brilliant footballing brain. He played in a more forward position in season 1956-57 and responded by delivering 24 league goals.

He won Second Division Championship medals, five international caps, English League and Under 23 representative honours, all with Wednesday, and an FA Cup Winners' medal with Manchester United a few years later in 1963.

Quixall played his first England international game in 1954 against Wales and within the space of 14 months had won another five caps, including one for the thrilling game against

Albert Quixall (Sheff Wed & England)

the European Select XI at Wembley in October 1953. England managed a creditable 4-4 draw thanks to a last minute penalty by full back, Alf Ramsey, the same chap who 13 years later managed to win England the World Cup.

Even after all his success at club and international level, when Harry Catterick took over Sheffield Wednesday he didn't look at Albert Quixall in the same light as the adoring Hillsborough crowd. So on September 18th, 1958 within one month of being appointed manager he sold Albert to Manchester United for a then record fee of £45,000. This initially turned many fans against Catterick, but to be fair to the man he did build a side that in his time at Hillsborough, nearly three years, did well. Wednesday achieved FA cup quarter and semi finals, won promotion as champions of division two and 2nd in the first division. Perhaps Catterick was right, but in the side that finished second to the double winning Tottenham Hotspur side I would have loved to have seen Albert alongside Tony Kay in midfield. We may just have had a championship winning season in the old memory banks.

Albert went on to play for Manchester United for just short of six years and appeared in the 1963 cup final winning side. He had his good times at Manchester scoring 51 goals in 165 outing, but never again scaled the heights he reached at Sheffield Wednesday.

In 1964 Albert asked for a transfer and United agreed but, unfortunately, no first or second division clubs showed interest. He went to Oldham and shortly afterwards on to Stockport County. At least in his last season as a player, 1966-67 his team managed to win the fourth division title.

Wednesday

Kind Regards
Albert Julian

Alan **Finney**

Alan Finney (Sheffield Wednesday)

Alan Finney was that old fashioned type of winger, the one who could cross a ball from the wing, cut inside and lay a pass direct to his own man, and still weigh in with eight to ten goals a season. The present day wingers, like Giggs, Anderton, Duff and Gronkear are held in such high esteem as well as costing tens of millions. It all seems a little unreal, count the number of goal that list got between them in one season and you wouldn't use all the digits on both hands. Alan Finney would, surely, be worth a few bob in today's game. He always seemed to find time and space to take the ball and get it under control, he seemed able to take on and beat a man and could then whip in a cross or have a crack at goal. When he was playing on the right wing and Colin Dobson played on the left, circa 61-65 seasons, it seemed to me to be the perfect balance for the side. With Layne and Fantham scoring regularly and the two wingers, between them, knocking in 20 plus goals a season, it was wonderful to watch.

Alan Finney started his first team career with Wednesday in February 1951 and played for 15 years appearing in over 500 league and cup games and scoring nearly 100 goals. His last game for Sheffield Wednesday was in their cup final season of 1966. In all the 16 seasons he played for the Owls he always managed to get his name on the scoresheet. Even in his last season when he only played 3 games he still popped in a goal.

Alan Finney was never capped at full international level, which still amazes me to this day. If Bryan Douglas of Blackburn and Edwin Holiday of Middlesborough (later of Sheffield Wednesday) could get selected, Douglas regularly, then surely Finney should have been a regular in the England side.

He did get some international recognition gaining under 23

caps against Italy in 1954 and Scotland in 1957. He was also selected as an England B player in 1956, this was also against Scotland.

Alan gave great service to Sheffield Wednesday and to prove my point of how good a winger he really was just look at the following list of players he supplied goalscoring opportunities for. I do believe prolific goalscorers need that supply of quality balls to develop the chances.

He played alongside Dooley 49 goals in one season - the highest ever by a Wednesday man. He played alongside Fantham, 147 league goals in his career - the highest postwar total. He supplied Froggatt 140 league goals in his career - the second highest postwar total. He also helped Roy Shiner 28 goals in a season and in the mid 1960s David Layne 29 goals in a season. Along with Quigley, Sewell and Quixall all 20 plus goals in a season.

Some winger that Finney!

When Alan Finney's career ended at Sheffield Wednesday he went the way of most higher league players and dropped down a couple of division but still decided to play his football locally. He moved to Doncaster Rovers where he won a championship medal for winning the fourth division title.

Alan actually made 455 league appearances, 39 FA Cup appearances and 9 Fairs Cup appearances. He scored 89 or 90 goals, depending on which records you use. I think he is marked down as having scored in the 1961-62 season Fairs Cup in some records.

He was a wonderful player who gave this supporter many years of enjoyment and a personal understanding of how wing play should be.

Thanks Alan, it was great to have seen you play for Sheffield Wednesday.

In his early years at Hillsborough when not selected for any of the teams or with no games to play that weekend, he was allowed to play for his old side Armthorpe Youth Club, Doncaster.

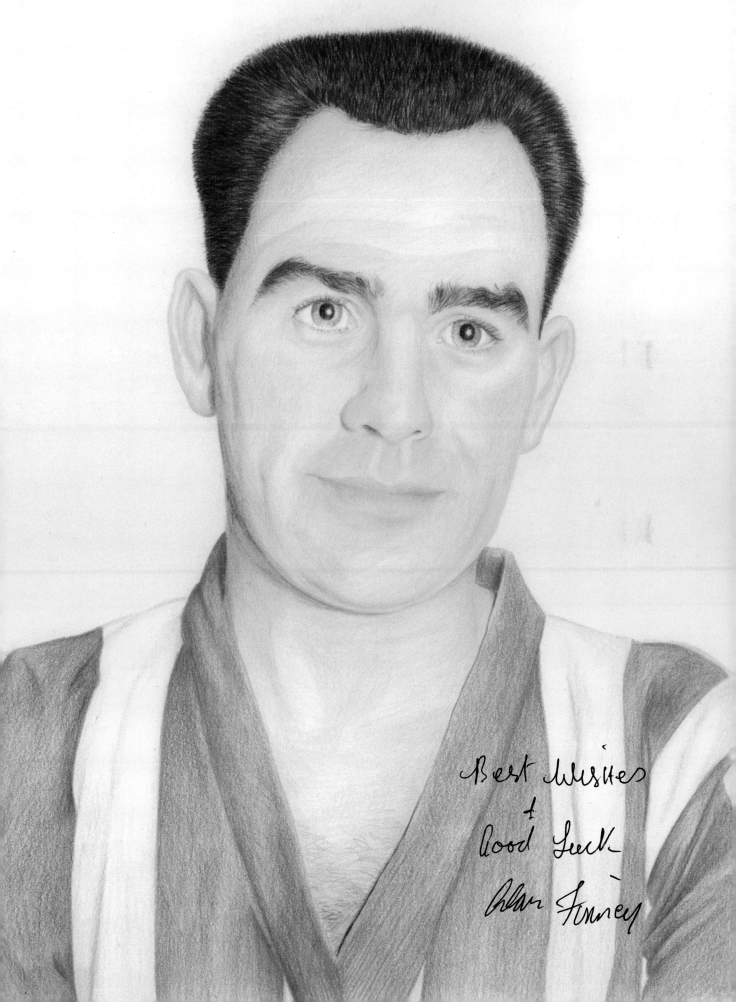

Best Wishes
&
Good Luck
Alan Finney

Tony **Kay**

Where do you start with Tony Kay?

He was a brilliant schoolboy player for Shirecliffe School who was signed by Wednesday and went on the make his debut in April 1955, aged 18. He played over 200 games for the Owls and was a wing half who had enough venom in him to excite the home crowd. They loved his every move and in equal measure he could rile the away supporters into howls of abuse at his tigerish tackling.

Tony should have been in the England World Cup Winning side of 1966 but somewhere along the line it all went very, very, wrong.

In 1964/1965 he, along with David Layne and Peter Swan were all charged with bribery. The match in question was against Ipswich. I recall reading a Sunday People article of their activities and said to my father "this could cause some problems". What an understatement. The newspapers, radio and television could not get enough of the scandal. The Football Association banned all of them immediately and a court case soon followed. All three of the players were subsequently jailed. They served their short sentences and were sine die, (banned) from playing any football for life. Eight years later in 1972 the three players had the ban lifted, but only Swan came back to make any more football league appearances. With the exception of his family, I don't think anyone ever knew where Tony Kay went to after his jail sentence was over.

Tony Kay (Sheffield Wednesday & England)

Swan stayed in football with Sheffield Wednesday, Bury and then into management at Matlock. He also kept a pub, the Travellers, down Attercliffe, where I was a regular customer. Layne, I think, had a couple of public houses in the Sheffield area and kept the Crown Inn on Meadow Hall Road for some time. But of Tony Kay I never saw or heard of him again.

The scandal of the bribes case does somewhat take away the height which Tony Kay scaled in the game of football. He was a brilliant ball player, with the ability to win the ball in midfield and pass it, long or short, to his own men. He could make runs forward and worry the opposition defence and had the ability to be a resolute defensive player when needed. If he had stayed away from the scandal of the bribery situation, he would, I am certain, have been in the England World Cup winning side. Nobby Stiles was selected for the '66 side, no disrespect to "Old Nobby" but I don't think he ever hit a pass over ten yards or made a run further than the halfway line. In fact the only goal I ever saw Stiles score, was at Hillsborough, and that was into his own net. It was, somehow, credited to Jack Whitham on the day Manchester United lost 5-4 at Hillsborough.

Kay had played a few first team games before Harry Catterick came to Hillsborough but it was the new manager who moulded Tony into the player we all loved. The work Catterick put into developing Kay paid dividends, he was an ever present in seasons 1960-61 and 1961-62, reached the semi final of the FA Cup, gained seven under 23 caps and represented the football league on three occasions as well a gaining a first division runners-up medal.

Kay played every league game and six cup games in 1961 when they achieved their second place behind the mighty Tottenham Hotspur. This was their highest league position since 1930 and it has not been bettered or matched since.

Catterick moved on to Everton and within months came back for his star midfielder paying Wednesday £55,000, then a record fee for a half back. Once again under the wing of his old manager, Kay produced brilliant displays and in his first full season was made captain and took Everton to the League Championship. This was followed by selection for the full England side against Switzerland, a debut game in which he also scored a goal.

Wednesday

Best Wishes

Sheffield

Peter **Swan**

"Swanny" as he was affectionately known by the supporters played his football in the best Wednesday defence for the last 60 years. Over the six full seasons he was a regular in the Sheffield Wednesday defence, 1959-1964, they averaged only 1.4 goals against, per game. He formed a great understanding with Ron Springett at club and England international level. They along with Megson, Johnson, McAnearney and Kay formed what must have been the tightest unit in the English First Division, which was the elite league, no Premiership in those days.

Peter Swan started his Wednesday career in May 1952, but had to wait for his league debut until 1955 when he played away against Barnsley in a 3-0 victory. He played in about 20 games over the next two seasons and in season 1958-59 he really established himself as a permanent fixture in the centre of

Peter Swan (Sheff Wed & England)

defence. It was in his first full season that Sheffield Wednesday won the 2nd Division championship. In the next five seasons he played more or less every league game and with the defence at its best in 1960-61, only 47 goals conceded in 42 games, the team won runners-up spot to Tottenham Hotspur. This was the least goals against tally in the football league that season. The next three seasons produced top six finishes and saw him take his total of England caps to 19, including the games leading up to the 1962 World Cup where he contracted tonsillitis and was replaced by Maurice Norman of Spurs. He played for the England under 23's on three occasions and also represented the English League.

Pete Swan was the type of defender every side likes to

have, big, strong, and athletic and with plenty of skill on the ball. He could stand up to the big lads Bobby Smith of Spurs, Derek Kevan of West Bromwich Albion, and also deal with the fast nippy types Barry Bridges of Chelsea and Jimmy Greaves of Chelsea, then Spurs. He was very rarely troubled too much by the opposition forwards, but I remember Doc Pace of Sheffield United invariably seemed to have a good game against him.

Unfortunately for Pete, Sheffield Wednesday and the fans, he was one of the players caught up in the bribes scandal, in 1964, for which he was banned from the game, for life. In 1972 the Football League lifted this ban and he promptly returned to professional football with his old club. He made another 15 appearance in the 1972-73 season for the Owls and then went in to the lower divisions with Bury and then to non league football with Matlock. As the manager of Matlock he achieved a Wembley win in the FA amateur cup final.

I, personally, remember Pete from his days as the landlord of the Travellers down on Attercliffe Road. We used to spend our dinner hour in his pub playing darts and having a couple of pints. He was a good landlord and excellent company, with a ready wit and an answer for everything.

He achieved over 300 appearances for Sheffield Wednesday covering 17 years and 7 day.

Conjecture abounds in football - but what if Swan and Layne had not been banned. Both these players were on top of their game when the scandal hit and Wednesday were a top six finisher for the five previous seasons. Swan was only 27 and reportedly on the verge of claiming his England place back. Layne was younger at 24 and being touted to gain honours after his two seasons of scoring 30 and 28 goals in season 62-63 and 63-64 respectively. Even under Alan Brown's poor guidance I am sure they would have been a formidable force for the rest of the sixties. Who knows, a championship may well have been within their grasp.

Wednesday

Johnny **Fantham**

I used to stand on the spion kop as an nine year old and hear supporters all around me shouting "gerrup linoleum". For a few years I just went along and sometimes even shouted this chant myself, never understanding what it meant. My father later told me it was because he was always sprawled out on the floor, so for a few years I knew John Fantham as "lino".

It must be said this was a slightly unfair nickname for a man who holds the postwar scoring record for Sheffield Wednesday with 147 league goals, with all but 12 of these being scored in the top division.

He was obviously highly thought of by Harry Catterick who had him earmarked to take the place of Manchester United bound Albert Quixall. This could have been too big a burden for some players, following the Golden Boy of Sheffield football, but John Fantham took it in his stride and very quickly won over all of the Owls supporters, even the ones who had called him "lino".

I recall Fantham being good in the air with a rasping shot and very, very fast over a short distance, basically, the type of guy you love as one of your strikers. His highest one season tally was, 24 goals, in season 1961-62, which included his first hat-trick, against Birmingham City. He was a fixture in the side for almost 12 years and in 10 of those seasons he scored into double figures, being the club's leading marksman on five occasions.

John, an ex Burngreave schoolboy, became an England international at the tender age of 22, when he was selected for a world cup qualifying match against Luxembourg on Thursday, September 28, 1961 at Highbury. The attendance of 33,409 included a young 12 year old who went all the way to London to see three of his favourite team play in a World Cup qualifier. Peter Swan and Ron Springett also played in the match that England won 4-1.

I actually thought Fantham had a quite good game and was well worth another chance, but the powers that be at the FA, did not agree and this was to be Fantham's only full England Cap. John was left in the international wilderness when some players around that era were scoring less goals per season and gaining far more caps.

Fantham did gain other honours: English League representative games against Italy and Ireland, under 23 caps, FA cup runners up medal, League runners up medal and a second division championship medal all added to John's excellent career.

John Fantham (Sheff Wed & England)

His Sheffield Wednesday career started on 1st of February 1958 and ended on 20th September 1969 and contained 147 Football League goals, 11 FA Cup goals, 4 League Cup goals, and 5 Fairs Cup goals in a total of 426 matches.

John Fantham equalled Redfern Froggatt's post war scoring achievement of 140 goals when he scored against the old enemy Sheffield United.

After his excellent service to Sheffield Wednesday he was sold by Danny Williams to Rotherham United, a club his father previously played wing half for, for a fee of £5,000. He went on to make another 51 football league appearances. He had a short spell at Macclesfield before retiring from football to become a respected businessman in the Sheffield area.

As a youngster I used to contact the photographers who were credited with taking pictures of the Sheffield Wednesday players. Their photographs appeared in all the football magazines of the time: Soccer Star, Football Monthly, a little magazine called Soccer, plus many more. But I can always remember Johnny Fantham's pictures were always that bit more athletic or acrobatic than the other players, overhead kicks, flying headers, walloping a thunderous shot onto goal.

Wednesday

Sheffield

Don **Megson**

"The best left back in England", no, not my words, but those of the legendary Liverpool Manager Bill Shankly, and if he thought so, who's to argue. Don Megson arrived, age 16, to start his Sheffield Wednesday career, in October 1952, from a Cheshire League side, Mossley. His preferred position was playing on the left wing. In his seven years of trying to get into the first team he played in every position, except goalkeeper, for the reserves. His breakthrough came under, that man again, Harry Catterick, who selected him at left back on 14th November 1959. Throughout the next 11 seasons, Don Megson figured in another 441 games for the Owls, nearly all in the left back position. Don Megson, to my limited knowledge, is the only Sheffield Wednesday player who has played over 400 games and not had to display his football prowess for the club outside of the top division.

After a couple of seasons he succeeded Tom McAnearney as captain and did the job brilliantly. In my time of watching Sheffield Wednesday, only Nigel Pearson has come anywhere near to Megson as a leader of his team. He had such a will to win, if things weren't going well, we had fallen a goal behind, had a player dismissed, or there was just a drop in the Owls performance, he'd be at the touchline asking for something from us, the supporters. Now I have no idea why the other 30,000 or so raised their voices another 25%, but I did it because I felt involved, I could help. It may sound naive but so what. He also did not leave it at crowd control, I have seen him give a verbal blast to the internationals in the side: Springett, Swanny and Fantham when they did

Don Megson (Sheffield Wednesday)

not live up to the Megson criteria. His son Gary, years later, had the same type of attitude to players who did not seem to be putting everything into the 90 minutes.

Don Megson was highly rated throughout the football fraternity, as indicated by Shankly's remarks, but the only recognition he ever received was one Football League appearance against the Italian League in 1960.

The memory most Sheffield Wednesday fans have of Megson is him leading the side around Wembley on May 14th, 1966, after the 3-2 defeat by Everton (why do I still hate Everton more than Manchester United). Old Harry Catterick, then manager of Everton, had his lucky charm with him that day. The Owls went 2-0 up on 58 minutes and looked to be in complete control. They sat back a little and paid an immediate price. Mike Trebilcock, definitely the manager's lucky charm, popped two goals in and a third by Derek Temple killed Wednesday off. In my mind the sheer disappointment of that one match echoed through the next four seasons: 11th, 19th, 15th, 22nd and relegated.

Megson only played 6 games in the 1969-70 relegation season and duly moved into player-coaching with Bristol Rovers. After a couple of seasons he was made manager and gained promotion to Division 2, and also won the Watneys Cup. He left Rovers in 1977 and took up a position to coach Portland Timbers in the North American Soccer League (NASL). After a successful spell in the States, Don came back to England to manage Bournemouth Football Club.

Don Megson played 442 games for the Owls and scored seven goals. Megson's last match for Sheffield Wednesday was in the FA Cup against Scunthorpe.

Megson appeared in 15 Sheffield Derbies, a higher number than any post war Owl, with five wins, five losses and five draws which also proved how tight the local games were.

Wednesday

Ron **Springett**

Ron Springett was the player who I idolised during his career at Hillsborough and was without doubt the best goalkeeper Sheffield Wednesday have ever had. Thirty-three England caps, all gained whilst playing for Sheffield Wednesday, is a record not bettered by any other Englishman who played for the Owls.

Springett was playing for Queens Park Rangers in the mid 1950s and was spotted by Eric

Ron Springett (Sheff Wed & England)

Taylor and transferred, for £9,000, to Hillsborough in March 1958. The nine year period from Springett being purchased to his departure in 1967 was probably Wednesday's most lucrative in league placings and cup runs. In Ron's first season, Sheffield Wednesday won the second division championship which, obviously, gained them promotion to the first division. Once back in the top flight they finished: fifth in 1960; second in 1961; sixth in 1962; sixth in 1963 and sixth again in 1964.

In the season they finished second to the great Tottenham Hotspur double winning side, 1960-61, Wednesday's points total would have been sufficient to have given them the title in both the season before, and the season that followed.

In 1960, they were unlucky to lose an FA Cup semi-final to Blackburn Rovers and in 1966 they went one better and reached the cup final.

Unfortunately, three seasons of finishing in sixth spot was deemed to be underachieving and the manager, Vic Buckingham, who had been in charge, was sacked. Personally, I think the next manager, Alan Brown, was the beginning of the demise of Sheffield Wednesday as a force in English football. He arrived in, July 1964, league positions dropped and even though Wednesday managed a Cup Final appearance in 1966

the writing was on the wall. He sold skillful players and replaced them with runners. But worse than all of the above he sold Ron Springett. In a unique deal with QPR, Ron's younger brother, Peter, came to Sheffield Wednesday with the elder Springett moved back to his old club in London.

So by the time Brown left in February 1968, the Owl were in 19th place in division one and had just missed relegation.

Ron Springett played for another three or four seasons with QPR and they managed to get promotion into division one and also had a couple of good FA cup runs.

Along with Lee Froggatt, a close friend, I went to Loftus Road, QPR's ground, to see Ron play his first game for them. This was in season 1967-68 and it did mean we missed the first game of the season at Hillsborough so much was our respect toward Ron Springett. He was definitely sold too early.

Ron Springett won 33 England caps, appeared in two world cup campaigns - one as winner, a runners-up league championship medal, a runners-up cup final medal, a second division champions medal, played 10 games in European Club competition and played for the English League on nine occasions. His association with Wednesday was very fruitful for both parties.

Springett's international career began in 1959-60 season when he won his first cap. Two seasons later and still first choice for his country he played in all of the games in the 1962 Chile World Cup Finals. His reserve in that campaign was Alan Hodgkinson of Sheffield United, another fine goalkeeper.

Ron remained first choice for England for a couple more years until Alf Ramsey came along. Oddly enough, an international match played at Hillsborough, against France, was, I think, the last game Ron played as first choice. Gordon Banks was promoted to the England number one spot. Springett did play a few more times for his country but only when Banks was injured. He was in the squad as reserve keeper for England in their World Cup winning year of 1966.

Colin **Dobson**

Born in 1940, during the Second World War, in Middlesborough, Colin Dobson made his Wednesday debut in 1961. He could possibly have broken into the Wednesday first team earlier, he was on the Wednesday books from 1956, but insisted on finishing his shipbuilding apprenticeship.

Dobson was a tricky little ginger haired winger who had excellent ball skills and invariably weighed in with 10-12 goals per season. Dobson was a regular in the Owls first team for about five years playing over 30 games in every season from 1961 to 1966. I saw him take on the international full backs of the day and leave them sitting on their backsides in his wake. His close ball control was excellent and he was inventive with his skills, he did things I had never seen a player do before. We all talked of Johan Cruyft with his new tricks in the seventies, but Dobson had been doing the same thing years before in the early sixties. He caught the selectors' eyes in 1963 when he won two England Under 23 caps. Unfortunately, no further honours came his way.

During my teens Colin Dobson was the type of player I really wanted to emulate – I had a good start, I already had the small stature, the ginger hair, but, unfortunately, none of the skill. So it was Ron Springett I modelled my game on. Poor players invariably end up in goal.

Dobson's career, as well as Sheffield Wednesday's, went downhill under Allan Brown. Brown took over from Vic Buckingham and in two seasons had turned Wednesday from a regular top six team into a side struggling to ward off the drop. We had one bright moment in those darkening days; in 1966 the Owls reached the FA Cup Final. Colin Dobson played in three of the cup ties, all six were played away from Hillsborough, and funnily enough scored his only FA cup goal for Wednesday in that run, against Newcastle. How I wish Dobson had played in all six of the cup matches. Manager

Brown dropped Dobson for the semi-final against Chelsea, replacing him with Graham Pugh. The manager's decision was never questioned because Pugh scored the first of the two goals in the semi to send Wednesday through to Wembley. For the first time in 31 years, the Owls were to play on the hallowed turf of Wembley, so FA cup hysteria was rife in Sheffield and in all the euphoria Colin Dobson played his last game for Wednesday seven days before the Wembley Cup Final and seemed to slip away from Hillsborough almost unnoticed. A poor decision by Brown, for although Pugh was a willing runner he was never in the same footballing class as Dobson. Pugh did not have the guile, the trickery, the speed nor the ability to score goals at the ratio Dobson did. In fact, for a winger, Colin Dobson's' returns were excellent: 177 league game and 49 goals scored, almost a goal every third game. He played in five European Fairs Cup matches for the Owls and scored on two occasions, never looking out of place when up against teams such as Barcelona, Cologne, Werder Bremen and even Pele's Santos.

Colin Dobson (Sheffield Wednesday)

Colin Dobson joined Huddersfield Town in 1966 where he actually bettered his Sheffield Wednesday scoring record by notching 50 goals in his 149 appearances for Town.

Colin continued his career at Brighton and Hove Albion and finally Bristol Rovers where he once again teamed up with an old Wednesday team mate, the Bristol Manager, Don Megson. He amassed over 450 games in league and cup football and scored well over 100 goals for the four clubs he played for between 1961 and 1975.

He went into coaching and was very well travelled, he gave service to Coventry, Bristol, a two year spell in the Arabian Gulf, Aston Villa, Sporting Lisbon, Gillingham and Coventry for a second time.

It was my great pleasure to have seen Colin at his best.

Wednesday

Gerry **Young**

Gerry Young (Sheff Wed & England)

Gerry Young was born in Jarrow on 1st October 1936. Just over 18 years later he was signed by Sheffield Wednesday and within two years, 1957, made his debut for the Owls. Gerry gave Sheffield Wednesday fifteen seasons of effort and undying loyalty. For the first of those five seasons he could not get a regular first team position, mainly because the centre forwards berth he aspired to was taken by the likes of Shiner, Layne, and others who he could not displace. It was Vic Buckingham who moved Gerry into the half back position vacated by Tony Kays' move to Everton in 1962, and from that point on his first team spot was assured. He was an intelligent passer of the ball and perhaps with playing up front in his early career his passes to the forwards always seemed to find their mark. He was stout in the tackle, did not shirk anything, and still managed to find the net on a few occasions. In the period 1963 to 1969 he formed an excellent central defensive partnership with Peter Swan and then Vic Mobley. The latter pairing were both selected to play for England. Mobley was injured and could not play but Gerry did make his England debut against Wales in a 2-1 victory on November 1964. Mobley was never selected again but Young was called up for the next England game against Holland. Sadly a few days before he would have won his second cap, Gerry ruptured his thigh and missed a large part of the season and obviously his chance of furthering his international career. The powers that be on the international scene never selected Young again.

Gerry played nearly all his first team games for Wednesday in the first division. He made 345 appearances for Sheffield Wednesday, his only club, and scored 20 goals.

One of the things Gerry will always be inextricably linked with is, during the 1966 F A Cup Final, a long punt upfield came to him and unusually he failed to trap and control the ball. It squirmed away and, as he turned, Derek Temple was on it in a flash and raced on to beat Ron Springett in the Wednesday goal to notch Everton's third goal in their comeback from two nil down. Besides the terrible feeling of losing that game, which was hard enough to swallow, I remember Ron Springett walking up to Young as he lay devastated on the Wembley turf and rubbing his hair. From that point in the game I could not see too clearly as I remember watching the remaining few minutes through a veil of tears. Also from that point onwards I have had an everlasting dislike for Everton.

Gerry Young, it must be said was one of Wednesday's better players on that Cup Final Saturday afternoon. He was almost babysitting Sam Ellis, a young reserve centre half, with only ten first team games under his belt.

Vic Mobley had been injured in the Chelsea cup semi final at Villa Park and was unlucky to have to miss the final. Sam Ellis was thus selected and placed alongside Young at the centre of defence. Whilst Ellis did not play badly it must be said his inexperience left Young with the burden of picking up both Alex Young and Mike Trebilcock on too many occasions. So a little tiredness may have contributed to the lapse in Gerry's concentration near the end of that 1966 cup final.

A one club man, Gerry retired from playing in 1971, nearly 14 years after his first game, which was on the 2nd of March 1957, and went on to the Sheffield Wednesday coaching staff.

Gerry, left Sheffield Wednesday in 1975 along with the Manager Steve Burkinshaw who had guided (if that's the correct term) the Owls in to division three after gaining only 5 wins all season.

Gerry along with Johnny Quinn, another ex Sheffield Wednesday player, ran a sports store and trophy centre on Middlewood Road in the Hillsborough area for many years after they had both retired

Wednesday

David **Layne**

David (Bronco) Layne played, in 1954, alongside two future England internationals, one of whom was to win a World Cup winner medal 12 years later in 1966. David played alongside Gordon Banks and John Fantham for Sheffield Boys. He was to team up with Fantham eight years later with Sheffield Wednesday. All three went to local clubs: Fantham, selected as the best prospect, to Sheffield Wednesday, Banks to Chesterfield and Layne to Rotherham. Layne's career did not seem to be going too well at Rotherham and so he moved on to Swindon. He had an upsurge in his form and he notched 28 goals in 41 games he then moved on to Bradford City where he carried on at the same scoring rate of two goals every three games, notching 44 goals in 65 games. He was hot property at that time and thankfully Wednesday bought him for around £16,000. His scoring ratio actually improved, albeit slightly. He scored 30 goals in 42 games in his first season at Hillsborough and followed this up with another 28 goals in 39 games in his second season.

I never saw Derek Dooley play, so I cannot say who was the best leader of the line, but Dooley scored his stunning one season tally a division lower than Layne whose Wednesday goals were all scored in the top division. In 49 years of watching the Owls, David Layne was the best centre forward I have seen. I appreciate that is a big statement to make, but I have seen all of the others who have played, Lee Chapman, David Hirst, John Ritchie, Jack Whitham, Keith Ellis, John Hickton (a player who should have been kept at Hillsborough) and many more all of whom I admired and cheered on heartily. But I still say, David you were my top man.

Unfortunately his judgement off the field did not match his

David Layne (Sheffield Wednesday)

soccer abilities and he along with Peter Swan and Tony Kay now of Everton were banned for life for their part in the bribery scandal that rocked English football in 1964. When, eight years later the ban was rescinded David tried to re-establish his career at Hillsborough. It was doomed to failure and he never got back into the first team. He moved on to Hereford, and even after dropping down the divisions still did not manage to get a regular place. After four games with Hereford David retired from professional football.

What could have been?

The newspapers of the day, 1963, 1964, were putting his name up for selection as the new England centre forward. To be fair to David with that type of goalscoring record he merited a chance. In his two years as an Owl the team managed a very respectable 6th position in both seasons. In those two years he alongside Colin Dobson and John Fantham all scored into double figures. Have Sheffield Wednesday had three forwards accomplishing that feat in the years since? In 1962-63 season Wednesday did the double over Manchester United, won and drew with the old enemy, Sheffield United – Layne scored four goals in those two games against the Blades, beat Arsenal at Highbury, and also won and drew with, the best side of that era, Tottenham Hotspur – Layne notched two goals against both these North London giants.

In the following season, 1963-64, Layne carried on scoring against all the top clubs once again. Coincidentally his biggest tally against one club that season was four goals against Ipswich Town, the side implicated in the bribes scandal.

David went into the licensing trade in Sheffield and for a considerable time was the landlord of the Crown Inn near the junction of Meadow Hall Road and Weedon Street.

Layne and Gerry Young are the only two Wednesday players to score hat tricks in European football against DOS Utrecht and Roma respectively

By the way the nickname "Bronco" came from a sixties TV cowboy show starring Ty Hardin as Bronco Layne.

Wednesday

Peter **Eustace**

Peter Eustace, a local lad who played for Stocksbridge Works before becoming a Wednesday player, in my opinion, should have been 'a great'. He had arrogance, top class ball skills, a vision for the defence splitting pass, defensively solid and was always ready for any chance to have a pop at goal.

He was called into the England squad (but never gained a cap), he was named as one of the best midfielders in England between 1966-1969. He could hold the ball and spray passes all about the field to his team mates and one of his managers at Sheffield Wednesday, Danny Williams, stated "Peter Eustace was the best player I have ever worked with".

Unfortunately, Eustace's' best footballing years were to coincide with Alan Brown and Danny Williams being in charge at Hillsborough. As the team slipped into the bottom places in Division One, Eustace, at least, escaped the ignominy of that awful relegation in 1970 by being transferred to West Ham United for a fee in excess of £90,000. It must be said Eustace did not pull any trees up in East London, although I do recall on one occasion he scored a hat-trick from midfield for the Hammers. He stayed at West Ham for about two years before being loaned (back up North) to Rotherham United. Derek Dooley, then Wednesday manager, repurchased Pete for a knock down fee of £12,000. In his comeback season 1972-73 Eustace played 24 games and scored 4 goals.

Eustace had a span of 13 years from his first game, in August 1962 to his last game on March 29th 1975. In my memory he seemed to have been a permanent fixture for all those years but in reality he only played in 268 games, scoring 25 league goals and one league cup goal. Peter Eustace was one of my favourite players (hence his appearance in this book) he could make a 60 yard pass, but also get stuck in when needed and he had that God given talent so few have, he could find space. When he received the ball he was invariably free of opposition players so that in that initial split second the ball would be controlled and then passed, invariably, to a Wednesday player. Only John Sheridan has matched Eustace, in my time watching football at Hillsborough, in the ability to find that little bit of extra time and space before laying the ball off.

Eustace left Sheffield Wednesday in March 1975 for a spell at Peterborough United before going into coaching. This was with some success at Sunderland and in 1983 he was asked by Howard Wilkinson, an ex team mate, to return to Wednesday as coach, an opportunity he readily accepted. In his five years as coach, Wednesday gained promotion to Division One with a highest finish of 5th and also reached an FA cup semi-final.

In 1988, Howard Wilkinson was being coveted by a few clubs. One of them, Leeds, finally made him an offer he could not refuse. So the coach, Eustace, took over the reigns at Sheffield Wednesday. Unfortunately, Peter Eustace will probably be remembered, by some Owls fan, more for his 19 games in charge than for the fine service he gave as a quality player or as an excellent coach.

Bad management, bad luck with injuries, bad team selection, whatever the reasons Peter Eustace only lasted four months as manager of Sheffield Wednesday. The shortest managerial span in the club's history. He only gained two wins out of the 19 games played and was basically doomed to the managerial wilderness. He returned to club management at

Peter Eustace (Sheffield Wednesday)

Leyton Orient in 1991 where he stayed in command until 1994. At the time of going to print he is back at Sheffield Wednesday as their chief scout.

It cannot be easy to manage a club where you have been idolised as a player - just look at Derek Dooley, Danny Wilson, to a slightly lesser extent Trevor Francis and the recently departed Chris Turner.

We the supporters, are a fickle lot and top seasonal goalscoring hero or League Cup final winner does not carry any weight when results are going against us.

Wednesday

Tommy **Craig**

Tommy Craig was transferred to Sheffield Wednesday from Scottish Club Aberdeen on 12th May 1969. I am not sure who gave the go ahead to take the risk of £100,000 being spent on a teenager as Wednesday were managerless at the time. It was most probably Eric Taylor, just about every decision around that time was his.

Craig signed in mid 1969, just in time to play in the last game of the season against Tottenham Hotspur. If memory serves me correctly the game was a goalless draw, but Craig showed enough signs with those elegant left foot passes to make the crowd look forward to some good stuff from the little ginger-haired midfielder.

In his first full season with Wednesday he displayed an elegant touch and a range of defence splitting passes that should have helped secure their place in Division One. Unfortunately the rest of the team at that time were either

Tommy Craig (Sheff Wed & Scotland)

ageing or to be blunt just not good enough. The sound defence was no more. Ron Springett, Megson and Mobley had moved on, Gerry Young was coming to the end of his career and in midfield Eustace was sold to West Ham. Up front John Fantham the saviour, with his goals in so many seasons had come to the end of his top level career. The 1969-1970 season had few highlights for Wednesday fans. Tommy Craig, in my humble opinion, was the best player in the side that year. He played all but 2 league matches and scored 5 goals, only three behind the leading marksman Jack Whitham who finished on 8 league goals. It was a dismal season and Craig must have wondered what he had let himself in for. Out of the 42 league games played the

Owls only managed to win eight and draw nine, a dismal 25 points were gained and relegation was assured.

The rest of Craig's Wednesday career, another four years, was spent in the second division. He played some excellent football for Wednesday and scored 40 goals from midfield, no mean feat. He was sold by Steve Burtenshaw who, I have read somewhere, saw Craig as somewhat of a luxury and decided to sell his only star player in December 1974 to Newcastle United. Soon afterwards Wednesday had dropped another division and even darker days were to follow at Hillsborough.

The fee for Craig was £120,000. In his three years at St James Park he played in 124 games and scored 22 goals. I recall seeing him put pass after pass into Malcolm Macdonald's path for the big centre forward to smash home. Craig's game, with that left foot pass just over or through the defence was tailor-made to work with a fast front runner like MacDonald and this was confirmed when he moved on to Aston Villa and made the same sort of chances for Andy Gray, which he, also, gleefully accepted.

In the latter part of his playing career he appeared for Swansea and Carlisle United before retiring and taking up management, with Hibernian in the Scottish League.

Craig gained Scottish youth caps, under 23 caps as well as full international honours.

I personally remember Craig as a hard working midfielder, brilliant on the ball, not too hot at tackling, it must be said, a very good free kick or corner taker and in the role of playing well upfield just behind the front men, whom he supplied numerous chances. He was excellent. Unfortunately for Wednesday and Craig there were no front men at that time who really took the chances he made. The best of this era was Brian Joicey who scored 48 goals in three full seasons, Mick Prendergast was second highest with 36 in four seasons and Tommy himself was third highest scorer with 30 goals over four seasons.

Wednesday

Terry **Curran**

Terry Curran was a brilliant little winger who in his time at Hillsborough could amaze and disappoint in equal measures. He had already been at five other clubs before he came to Wednesday in March 1979 from Southampton and to be fair he made it straight to the hearts of the Wednesday faithful. In his first full season, the Owls gained promotion from the third division, and Curran was possibly the central figure in that campaign. His 22 league goals were a real bonus from a player who never actually played as an out and out striker. He was given a roaming or free role to play and did this to great effect. In Curran's three full seasons at Sheffield Wednesday he gained promotion in season 1979-80, and finished 10th and 4th respectively, in the next two season, just missing out on promotion.

Curran scored 35 league goals and 4 league cup goals for Sheffield Wednesday and I along with most Owls fans would select one of his tally which was better than all the other 38. It was at Bramall Lane in the promotion season of 1979-80 and Wednesday were 1-0 down and the Blades fans were loving it. Over to Terry, he picked up the ball out on the left, adjacent to the corner flag and set off on a run that I can still vividly recall, even now. He beat at least two men, and made directly for the United goal, he then released a shot which entered the top corner giving the Blades keeper no chance. We were ecstatic, and more than half of a 45,000 crowd went wild. This was the second meeting of the Sheffield clubs, the first meeting of that season was over the Christmas holiday. Yes, the Boxing Day massacre was a great day and another goal for Curran who was one of four scorers as the Owls gave the fans the best possible Yuletide present.

Terry Curran's next two seasons with Wednesday were no where near as profitable. He made 35 league appearances in both 1980-1981 and 1981-1982 seasons, but only scored 11 and 3 goals respectively, a lesser return than we had come to expect. To be fair to Terry he was asked to play a more disciplined role, taking on more specific duties, something that Curran was not able to do and his form deteriorated.

Even though he, surely, must have been able to see Wednesday were on the up, he made somewhat of a sensational decision to seek a transfer. It was bad enough that a player who was hero worshiped by the fans had asked for a move, but the team he decided on going to was the real problem, Sheffield United. What made the matter worse was the fact that the two clubs could not agree the fee and a tribunal decided. The financial outcome was a lot lower than Wednesday's expectations and was compounded by the fact that a year later Curran was sold on to Everton for a considerable profit. To be fair to Curran he was playing a higher level of football and within 18 months had gained a league championship medal with the Toffeemen in season 1984-85.

Terry was soon on the move again and by the end of his career he had played for 13 different clubs.

I personally thought Terry Curran should have reached greater heights, but a little bit of a problem with authority and a willingness to always speak his mind, not a bad thing in general, but in football it did hinder his career.

Curran was a very volatile character and in one game at Oldham he was involved in a clash with Simon Stainrod. In the ensuing uproar, 20 people, including police, were injured. Fans hurled concrete, bricks, coins - anything they could find. The scenes brought tears of frustration to the eyes of Big Jack as he pleaded, unsuccessfully, for restraint.

Terry Curran (Sheffield Wednesday)

Wednesday

Terry Curran

Mel **Sterland**

"Zico" as he was affectionately known to the Wednesday fans came directly to Sheffield Wednesday from Wealtheof School, where he played football for the school with the artist of this book, Gary Mackender. Mel and Gary also played for the local pub team, the Three Feathers, which is situated on Prince of Wales Road.

Sterland started life at Hillsborough as a midfielder, he made his debut playing in that position at the end of 1978-79 season, aged only 17, as a substitute against Blackpool and also played his first full game in the last match of the season against Hull City, a game in which he scored in a 2-3 home defeat.

Season 1979-1980 faired little better for Sterland who only made two appearances both as substitute.

Season 1980-81 was his breakthrough year and he played 21 league games, albeit in five different positions.

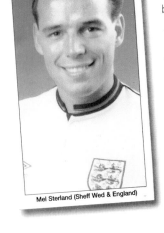

Mel Sterland (Sheff Wed & England)

He was converted to full back by Jack Charlton in season 1981-82 and made 29 appearances, 27 of them at right full back. From that astute managerial decision onwards Mel was to become one of the best full backs in English football for a decade. He also weighed in with more than his fair share of goals. In the Owls promotion season in 1984 he knocked in 9 goals. In the top flight of English football in season 1985-86 he did even better scoring an astounding 11 goals from his full back position, none of these strikes were penalties.

Sadly it took the FA until 1988 to realise that Sterland should be credited with an England cap, he gained that honour against Saudi Arabia. Mel Sterland was never selected to play for his country again.

His raids up the wing were a joy to behold and watching the opposition bounce off his bulky physique used to bring a collective cheer from all around the ground.

With 49 goals scored and nearly 350 games played Mel Sterland was relieved of the captaincy by the then manager Peter Eustace. It was possibly pride that made Sterland ask for a transfer and in March 1989 after Eustace had been dismissed and Ron Atkinson was in charge he was still allowed to be transferred to Glasgow Rangers. It was a brief but profitable stay at Ibrox and after nine games, which included three goals he gained a Scottish Championship medal. He was re-united with Howard Wilkinson who brought him to Leeds United in June 1989. In his first season at Leeds 1989-90 he gained promotion to the First Division. The following year 1990-91 he played every game of the season for the first time in his career. Season 1991-92 brought about the highlight of Mel Sterland's career: a League Championship Winners Medal. This was the last Division One Championship medal ever cast, as from the following season the Premiership came into being.

After the championship season Sterland carried an injury that required nine months lay-off from the game. He made his return but it only lasted five games and Leeds reluctantly terminated his contract in 1994. Sterland played in 146 games for Leeds United and scored 20 goals.

After his retirement from top class football Mel stayed in the game, albeit at a lower level, and went on to manage Boston United in the Unibond League in 1994. After two seasons Mel left the club in 1996, this despite leading them to second place in the League.

With over 500 league games and more than 80 goals scored, medals won for Scottish and English League Championships, England Under 21 European Champions, Mel Sterland had a wonderful 18 years in the game of football.

Wednesday

Peter **Shirtliff**

Peter Shirtliff joined Sheffield Wednesday directly from school in 1977 aged 16 and within his first year at the club had made his debut. In August 1978 Jack Charlton selected Peter to play in the Owls defence where he impressed. He made another 28 appearances that season. Jack Charlton, an ex centre half himself, obviously spotted something in Peter and as with most good managers realised age is not a problem, if the young man is good enough, play him. Peter played in 223 games for Wednesday in his first spell at the club which stretched from 1978 until 1986. He decided to leave the club when he no longer commanded a regular first team place. From 1984 he was up against the likes of Pickering, Lyons, Madden, Smith, Hart, and Ian Knight all vying for the two central defensive places. So in 1986 Peter took up the challenge with Charlton Athletic who had just been promoted to the top division. I recall in Shirtliff's first season at Charlton they ended up playing in the end of season play-offs to see who stayed in Division One. Charlton played Leeds United and were 1-0 down in extra time with just 7 minutes left. Peter scored 2 late goals that kept his side in Division One. In his next season at Charlton he was given the captaincy.

How things change in football. Ron Atkinson was now in charge at Hillsborough (1989) and he fancied Shirtliff to do a job for Wednesday in central defence and so he went out and bought back a player we transferred only 3 seasons earlier for £500,000, four times the amount we sold him for. Peter played in 33 games in season 1989-90 but unfortunately Wednesday were relegated.

The next season 1990-91 Peter played in 52 games for the Owls when promotion was gained and the first major trophy of any kind for 56 years was won at Wembley when we beat Manchester United 1-0. Along with Nigel Pearson, Shirtliff was outstanding in central defence and kept the highly rated Manchester forwards to hardly any clear cut chances on goal. I think Chris Turner only had one goalbound shot to save all afternoon.

Shirtliff only played 41 more games in the next two seasons due to injury. In season 1992-93 Peter was captain and around the Christmas period Wednesday went from 15th to 4th with a nine game run of seven wins and two draws. Sadly in the next game against Liverpool Peter broke his arm and was out for a couple of months which meant he missed the FA Cup semi-final against Sheffield United (by the way we won that game 2-1) and the League Cup final against Arsenal.

Shirtliff made his comeback from injury in early May and was hoping to be selected for the FA Cup final. He played with a cast on his broken arm and possibly trying to impress the manager overdid things and pulled a calf muscle which eliminated him from the Cup Final. With Nigel Pearson already missing with a broken leg injury the central defensive problem proved too much for Wednesday to overcome and for the second time in two months Sheffield Wednesday were beaten in a cup final by Arsenal.

Peter Shirtliff (Sheffield Wednesday)

Fully recovered and looking forward to playing alongside new signing, England defender, Des Walker in the 1993-94 season Peter was amazed to learn Trevor Francis had accepted an offer from Wolverhampton Wanderers of £250,000. He was duly transferred and had two good years at Molyneaux before being bought by his home town club, Barnsley were he played a significant part in their rise to the top flight, under his old team mate Danny Wilson.

Peter Shirtliff played in over 350 games for the Owls and was always a fine role model for the players around him. From his first game in 1978 to his last in 1993 his Wednesday career in two parts spanned 15 wonderful years.

Gary **Bannister**

Jack Charlton bought Gary Bannister from Coventry City for £100,000 at the beginning of season 1981-82. Although he had only scored three goals in his 22 appearances for the Sky Blues, Charlton must have seen potential in the player and took the risk. The risk duly paid off, Gary was an immediate hit with all the Wednesday fans. His 22 goals (21 in the league) played a big part in the Owls climb up the second division to secure 4th spot, only just missing out on promotion. If nothing else Gary was consistent, he notched 22 goals in all of his three seasons at Hillsborough. In 142 games played he scored 66 goals. A very respectable record.

He was voted the supporters Player of the Year for 1982, he helped Wednesday to the Semi Final of the FA Cup in 1983 and was prominent in the Owls gaining promotion in 1984.

Gary Bannister (Sheffield Wednesday)

All in all not a bad three years for Gary. Sadly, for The Owls, and, I think, in the long run for Bannister himself, he was transferred to QPR for £200,000 in 1984 before he had the chance to show his quality for Wednesday in the top flight.

In the three years I watched Gary Bannister play for the Owls he showed just how goalscoring chances should be taken. He was a selfish lad, of that there is no doubt, but so was Jimmy Greaves, Gary Linaker, Ian Wright, Michael Owen et al. To give Bannister his credit he did pop a lot of those chances in when all the crowd were yelling for him to pass it to a better positioned team mate.

For a while Jack Charlton played him up front with players like McCulloch and John Pearson both of them wholehearted triers but both only provided seven goals each in the 81-82 and 82-83 seasons. New manager Howard Wilkinson's introduction

of Imre Varadi in season 1983-84 seemed to spark life into the whole Wednesday team. Bannister contributed his 22 goals, Varadi scored 19 goals and another 12 Wednesday players pitched in with 48 more goals between them to gain promotion after 14 years in the lower division wilderness.

At this stage in his career, Bannister was still only 23 years of age and he seemed to have the football world at his feet. He was at a good club whose fans adored him. He seemed to have found a good partnership with another forward, Varadi, who could also knock 'em in. And to add to the mix he was going to play in the top division.

I will never understand why he thought a transfer to Queens Park Rangers would be a better bet than staying at Sheffield Wednesday.

To be fair he did have the chance to play in a League Cup final which they lost and he also scored 56 goals in 136 appearances. Not as prolific a record as when he was at Hillsborough but still a good strike rate.

Bannister left QPR and went back to Coventry City in March 1988 but it was not quite the success he hoped it would be. In his 43 games he scored only 11 goals and after two years he was transferred on to West Bromwich Albion. He stayed two seasons at the Hawthorns, playing 72 games and scoring 18 goals, he was loaned to Oxford United in this period and played 10 games scoring twice.

From WBA he moved on to Nottingham Forest on a free transfer. Luck was not really on Gary's side and in his first season with Forest, 1993, they finished bottom of the Premier League and were duly relegated. In his time at Forest Gary managed eight goals in 27 full appearances. After his spell at Forest, Bannister had short spells at Stoke City and Lincoln City before he became player coach at Darlington.

S h e f f i e l d

Gary **Megson**

Gary Megson (Sheffield Wednesday)

Gary Megson as you would expect from the son of an ex Sheffield Wednesday captain was an Owl through and through. He was brought up in Sheffield and has supported Sheffield Wednesday all his life.

His first taste of professional football was with Plymouth Argyle in October 1977 against local rivals Portsmouth. He was at Home Park for two years until November 1979 when Everton stepped in and purchased him for £250,000, a fee that broke Argyle's transfer record. After two years at Everton, Wednesdays' manager, Jack Charlton, stepped in and bought him for a very reasonable fee of £130,000. This started the first of Gary's two spells at Hillsborough. His first game was against Blackburn Rovers on August 29th 1981, a 1-0 victory, with Terry Curran scoring. This was followed by three more wins and Megson seemed to be settling in with the rest of his team very easily. With 20 wins and 12 draws it was a considerable improvement on the previous seasons and Wednesday managed fourth spot in the league just missing out on promotion. Megson played in all but two league games. The following season was more of the same but sixth position in the league was deemed a little bit of a let down. On the plus side we had the cup run to keep the excitement going up to April when we lost to Brighton in the FA Cup semi final. Gary Megson was the leading scorer in that cup run with 5 goals in 7 matches. The following season 1983-84, Gary played in all 42 league games, all 7 league cup games and 4 out of 5 FA cup games. Wednesday finished second in Division Two and were promoted to the top flight of English Football. Megson was then transferred to Nottingham Forest in a £175,000 deal that was nothing short of ludicrous. Wednesday should definitely have put up more of a fight to keep the best midfielder we had at that time. But even more bizarre was the fact that Forest never played Gary in the first team. A few years later Cloughie did something similar to John Sheridan who was also there for three months and never played a league game. Brian Clough may have been one of the country's best managers but he definitely missed out on two very good players for Nottingham Forest.

Gary Megson grabbed at a lifeline from Newcastle United who by this time were being managed by his old mentor Jack Charlton. Unfortunately for Gary, Charlton moved out almost at the same time and the new management did not have Charlton's belief in Megson. Wednesday went in to see if they could loan their former player back to Hillsborough. This was allowed and after a short spell Megson was once again a Wednesday player for a knockdown price of £60,000. His return coincided with the Owls best finish in the top division for over 25 years and another FA Cup semi final appearance. Once again Wednesday lost, this time, 2-1 to Everton, in fact this was the third semi final Megson had lost, he played in 1980 for Everton in their failed bid to make the final.

Megson played another two seasons with Wednesday before being transferred to Manchester City where he helped them gain promotion in his first season. In 1992 he was given a free transfer and joined Norwich City, a club he later managed for a short period. He also managed Stockport County and Blackpool. He is at present managing West Bromwich Albion in their struggle to consolidate a place in the Premiership.

Gary Megson was 10 years old in April 1970 when he was in the crowd at Hillsborough to see the Owls lose 2-1 to Manchester City and get relegated to the second division. By coincidence he was a member of the Wednesday side who clinched promotion 14 years later in 1984

It was a pleasure to have watched two generations of Megsons put their all into the Sheffield Wednesday cause.

Wednesday

Nigel **Worthington**

Nigel Worthington was one of those players who seemed to have to do that bit extra to impress the Hillsborough crowd. He had his detractors or as some would call them boo boys. For a few years when Worthington came to Sheffield Wednesday I would walk away from the ground and hear some people (fans, I think) saying Worthington had cost this and done that wrong. It took Nigel Worthington about two or three years to win the Hillsborough fans over. This he did and proved to be one of Sheffield Wednesday's finest defensive players of the last twenty years.

Worthington was brought into English football, from Irish club Ballymena, by Jimmy Sirrel in June 1981 to play for Notts County at Meadow Lane, who at the time were coached by, Sheffielder, Howard Wilkinson.

Two years later, in June 1983, Wilkinson was installed as the new Wednesday manager after the departure of Jack Charlton and one of his early signings was Worthington in February 1984 for £125,000. Nigel played in the last 14 games of the promotion season and scored a very important only goal of the game away against Huddersfield.

For the next 10 years Nigel Worthington was a first team regular except for a short period in 1986 when after an injury he could not regain his place in the team and only played 15 games that season.

In Sheffield Wednesday's promotion year Nigel won the first of his Northern Ireland caps against Wales in the Home Internationals. He gained 49 more international caps with the Owls. A record haul of caps by an individual whilst with Sheffield Wednesday. In 1986 he achieved a feat not many Wednesday players have had the privilege of doing, he played in the World Cup finals in Mexico.

Worthington played through some of the best years the Owls have produced in my time visiting Hillsborough:

In '84 they gained promotion; '85, finished 8th in Division One; '86 finished 5th in Division One, as well as reaching the FA Cup semi-final; '91 gained promotion back to Division One and beat Manchester United in the Rumbelows (League) Cup Final; '92 finished 3rd in Division One (highest finish for nearly 30 years; '93 played in European Competition also for the first time in nearly 30 years and appeared in the FA cup final and League cup final. Also in 1993 they made four appearances at Wembley, League Cup Final - Semi-final against the Blades - FA Cup Final - FA Cup Final replay.

After more than 10 years' loyal service, Howard Wilkinson, now installed as Leeds Manager, paid Wednesday £325,000 for Worthington's services. This had to be seen as good business for Trevor Francis and the Owls, a player nearly 33 years of age for a fee of that size.

Nigel once again gave good service to his new club, but with Tony Dorigo and Gary Speed playing on the left his outings were restricted to filling in when either of these players were injured or finding himself on the substitutes' bench. In all, he made 53 league and cup appearances and after his two year contract was completed he left Leeds United to become player manager of Blackpool.

Nigel Worthington (Sheff Wed & N Ireland)

He is now manager at Norwich City and at the time of this book going to press is facing a hard fought battle to keep his side in the Premiership. I really do hope he succeeds.

Lee **Chapman**

Lee Chapman was bought as a replacement for Gary Bannister in July 1984. He was purchased from Sunderland, who were managed at the time by ex Wednesday manager Len Ashurst, for £100,000. Chapman had the background to be a class act. His father, Roy, who played for Forest, scored around 200 goals in just over 400 games, so something along those lines would do for the Owls. To be fair to Chapman he was not far off that ratio in his four full seasons at Hillsborough. He scored 78 goals in 181 games, that's a goal in every 2.3 games.

Chapman played for Stoke schoolboys and he went on to make nearly 107 appearances for Stoke City where he notched 38 goals. He was transferred to Arsenal in 1982, for £500,000, but this was not an ideal move for Chapman and due to an untimely cartilage operation he was never an automatic choice. In December 1983 he was bought by Sunderland, this move was another that did not work out for Chapman and the move to Hillsborough was a lifeline he gratefully accepted.

Gary Bannister, the man Chapman was brought in to replace, was idolised by the fans and this big, 6ft 2inch ex Arsenal bloke was not going to find replacing him easy. It was not love at first sight but slowly and surely Chapman battled his way through the Hillsborough discreditors as well as the opposition defences. By the end of his first season he had notched 20 goals, only 2 short of Bannister's regular haul. His next season was not quite as prolific, only 15 goals, he was restricted, through injury, to 29 league games. His next two seasons 1986-87 and 1987-88 were even better, 22 and 21 goals respectively. So what Howard Wilkinson had done was to let a prolific goalscorer go to QPR for £200,000 and brought in an equally prolific scorer for £100,000. Good business and let's not forget Chapman was doing the business at a higher level of football.

One of his goals, against Arsenal, ranks fairly high on my list of great goals I have seen at Hillsborough, and it must have made Chapman feel rather good as it was against one of the clubs who discarded him earlier in his career.

In his four seasons at Hillsborough he proved not only to be a good target man, very powerful in the air, but also more adept on the ground than most people gave him credit for. It was a great pity, in May 1988, when he moved away from Hillsborough to a French club, Niort. The actual transfer deal became rather surreal when it was discovered that Niort could not pay the modest transfer fee. There was a period where Chapman was in limbo until Nottingham Forest came in and purchased him. His first season at Forest was very productive, his goals helped Forest secure third place in Division One and produce a League Cup and Simod Cup double. Surprisingly they sold him to Leeds, in January 1990. Managed by Howard Wilkinson, who knew Chapman's pedigree from four excellent seasons at Wednesday, he used

Lee Chapman (Sheffield Wednesday)

Chapman to spearhead the final tilt at promotion from Division Two in 1990. Promotion to the top division was gained and within two seasons Leeds, under Wilkinsons' guidance, had secured the first division championship. Chapman came back to haunt Wednesday in Leeds Championship winning season, scoring a hat-trick at Hillsborough. At the end of the next season, 1992-93, Chapman was put up for sale by Leeds and he joined Portsmouth, but within one month was playing for West Ham United. He later signed for Ipswich Town before returning to Leeds United to play just two games before joining Swansea City on a free transfer.

Married to the actress, Lesley Ash, Lee now runs a wine bar in London.

Wednesday

David **Hirst**

David Hirst was 17 years old when Sheffield Wednesday signed him from his home town club Barnsley in 1986. He had made 28 appearances for Barnsley with a decent return of nine goals.

Allan Clarke the Barnsley manager sold Hirst to Wednesday for £200,000 with a clause of another £50,000 if Hirst ever claimed a full international cap (which he did in 1991).

David's first knowledge of this move came when Clarke summoned him to his office and announced he was now a Sheffield Wednesday player. This can not have gone down too well with Hirst who was Barnsley through and through and did not like the Owls at all.

David scored on his debut for the Owls against Everton in August 1986 and made another 20 appearances that season and scored six goals. His next two seasons were more of the same, 26 appearances - 4 goals, 35 appearances 9 goals. Not stunning returns for a centre forward. His luck changed when Ron Atkinson took over. Atkinson took some of the shackles off Hirst telling him to concentrate on what he did best and forget his previous instructions. This obviously worked because in Atkinson's time at Hillsborough, David notched over 50 goals for him.

Hirst hit 16 goals in Sheffield Wednesday's relegation season and followed that with 28 goals the following season when the Owls won promotion and went on to win the Rumbelows Cup at Wembley.

I have heard it stated that David scored 32 goals that season, but I cannot find the records that show this to be so.

David Hirst (Sheff Wed & England)

When David was in top form – he was one of the best young prospects in English football. He was scoring a serious amount of goals for Sheffield Wednesday and was selected to go on tour with the England Squad to Australasia in 1991. David gained three full international caps and scored one goal.

At the start of season 1991-92 David took just three minutes to get off the mark with a goal against Aston Villa. He managed another 20 goals that season and Wednesday finished in a highly respectable position.

It was around this time that, supposedly, a communication from Alex Ferguson had offered £4,000,000 for Hirst to be transferred to Manchester United. I wonder if that was true?

The next season was one of mixed fortune for David. A broken ankle inflicted by Bould of Arsenal ruined what could have been Wednesday's best season ever. With a fully fit Hirst rampaging around who knows what may have happened. But it was still a memorable season for Hirst. He scored his 100th goal for Wednesday in the Wembley Cup Final to secure a replay. He scored his first and only European competition goal. He took some part in all four Wembley appearances and scored 11 league goals in only 22 appearances. Not too bad for an injured striker.

Hirst injury problems are well documented and they did restrict his appearance for the Owls in the following two seasons. He was only making intermittent appearances for the Owls and it was not until the 1995-96 season he secured his 100th league goal against Everton, who coincidentally were the club he scored his first Wednesday goal against.

David Pleat was now in charge at Hillsborough. When Southampton tried to secure Hirst's services. Hirst decided that he did not figure in his new manager's plans he took up the challenge of a new club.

The goals Hirst scored for the Owls were a delight to have witnessed. Especially the one against Sheffield United at Bramall Lane.

Wednesday

Sheffield

Kevin **Pressman**

Kevin Pressman, who was born in Fareham in 1967, was playing for England Schoolboys when he was first seen by Sheffield Wednesday scouts and quickly signed by the club. Kevin slowly, but surely, made his way through the ranks to gain first team recognition before his 20th birthday.

He made his debut on 5th September 1987 when Martin Hodge was injured. By the end of that season he had forced his way past Hodge to become first choice. The following three seasons he vied with Chris Turner for the Wednesday goalkeeper's position.

When Pressman was injured against Manchester City, in 1990, Turner gained a foothold on the first team position and Pressman took a back seat for a while.

He was unfortunate in the fact that in their promotion and Cup winning season, 1991, he played for the first half of the season appearing 23 times in the league and in six games in the League cup.

To miss the final at Wembley was a real shock to the system for Pressman and he was even more devastated when Trevor Francis took over from Ron Atkinson as manager within weeks of the

Kevin Pressman (Sheffield Wednesday)

Wembley victory. Obviously, Trevor did not rate Pressman that highly and paid a large sum of money for the Glasgow Rangers keeper, Chris Woods. Towards the end of the 1991-1992 season Kevin was loaned out to Stoke City.

Francis had played at Glasgow Rangers with Woods and rated him highly, and after all, he was the incumbent England goalkeeper. I honestly think that Pressman was a better all round goalkeeper than Chris Woods, safer hands and definitely a better shot stopper, but the manager, initially, did not.

After two seasons of keeping the substitute bench warm, and only making seven appearances, Pressman forced his way past Woods and back into the first team. If he had only regained his place a few months ealier we may not have lost the FA Cup final replay, or been beaten twice by Sheffield United, all games where Woods seemed to lack confidence.

From that point onwards Kevin Pressman was the Sheffield Wednesday keeper. Czech keeper Pavel Srnicek gained the spot for some months in the 1999/2000 season, but after a long fight it was Pressman who came out on top and Srnicek left the club at the end of the season.

Pressman has been a professional at Hillsborough since the 1985/86 season and has notched up well over 400 appearances for the club. He has played for the England 'B' side and came close to gaining a full England cap.

With the goalkeeping position it is obvious that when mistakes happen it is highly likely to be more significant then losing the ball in midfield or up front. One slip, one dropped ball or slight lack of judgement by a keeper and it is most probably a goal against. Kevin Pressman did make some errors, as all keepers do, but his confidence in himself never waned. This is exactly what is needed from a man the whole team relies on.

When Chris Turner returned as manager of Sheffield Wednesday, Pressman must have feared the worst, an old goalkeeping rival coming in as boss. Turner looked to Preston North End to their reserve keeper, Lucas, to be the Owls' new custodian. Why try and mend something that is not broken.

Kevin Pressman was now surplus to requirements at Hillsborough and at the end of season 2003-2004 he left and decided to find another club who would value his services.

At the time of this book going to press, Kevin is first choice keeper at Leicester City, in a higher division, keeping England's Ian Walker out of the starting line-up. So perhaps we did release Pressman too early. A class keeper, who looks after himself, can go on until about the age of 40. Kevin is a class goalkeeper with a good few seasons left in him.

Nigel **Pearson**

Nigel Pearson was twenty four years old when he arrived at Hillsborough, having spent the earlier part of his football career with Shrewsbury Town football club. Howard Wilkinson saw something in Pearson when he played against Wednesday in two league cup matches and promptly bought him. My selection of Pearson is for his determination to win, he was what I would describe as a real football team captain.

I know the initial appointing of Pearson as captain was instrumental in Mel Sterland asking for a transfer and it caused a certain amount of bitterness with Nigel receiving letters from Owls fans stating their annoyance at the switch. But I think in all honesty, Peter Eustace, in his much maligned four months managerial career at Hillsborough made a brilliant tactical decision to move Pearson to team captain.

Nigel Pearson (Sheffield Wednesday)

Pearson led by example, he obviously made some mistakes but I found these were outweighed by his honesty and excellent leadership. He knew how to rally his team, especially at corners or set piece free kicks. In the promotion and Rumbelows Cup winning season Pearson more than led by example. He scored 12 goals in all that season and was the leading scorer in their successful cup run, with six goals – not bad for a central defender! Some of today's highly rated strikers would take a return of 12 goals in the season, ask Emile Heskey or Duncan Ferguson. The Wembley Cup Final win was the highlight of Nigel's career, with Wednesday, beating Manchester United, being voted man of the match all adding up to make it a very memorable day, indeed. I read in the Sheffield Star book "Wednesday, Every day of the week" that he treasures a little cut glass owl he had thrust into his hand by a little girl as he led his team on a lap of honour, during the league cup semi against Chelsea, stating "it means as much to me as my man of the match trophy" he received at Wembley. This is the type of connection with fans you don't seem to get from some of the present day players who only seem interested in their contractual rights, first team football or else, get out clauses, etc.

To be honest it must be great to be an Arsenal or Manchester United supporter especially over the last 15 years or so but I would imagine they have become somewhat blasé about winning. I cannot imagine they have the same tear jerking feeling as when you see a major trophy lifted by your team captain for the first time in your lifetime, and I was born in the forties! One decent trophy in my 50 years of visiting Hillsborough (division two titles excluded), but you could see on the face of Pearson when he lifted the trophy towards the fans it meant as much to him as it did to the supporters.

Nigel carried on being a leader of the team until he broke his leg in the semi-final against Blackburn Rovers, in 1993, and with Peter Shirtliff suffering from a broken arm the heart of the Wednesday defence was ripped out in their two finals against Arsenal. Carlton Palmer, Viv Anderson and Paul Warhust manfully tried their best, but the truth is you cannot lose the positional and leadership qualities of a Pearson or a Shirtliff.

After the awful double defeat by Arsenal, in the cups of 1993, Pearson only played six more games for the Owls and was transferred to Middlesborough in October 1993, exactly six years to the day since he arrived from Shrewsbury. Hindsight is a wonderful thing, but I really do think Trevor Francis sold Pearson, along with a couple of other players, too early. A point I think Nigel Pearson proved at Middlesborough, where, once again installed as team captain, he led them to two cup finals in 1997 and another Coca Cola cup final in 1998.

Nigel Pearson only played 217 games for the Owls but he, along with Don Megson, are the two best leaders of players I have ever had the pleasure of watching.

Carlton **Palmer**

Carlton Palmer started his football league career with West Bromwich Albion in September 1985, and was a first team regular for four years until Sheffield Wednesday stepped in and bought him for £750,000 in 1989. His ex manager Ron Atkinson obviously liked what he had seen of Carlton in his second stint as manager at the Hawthorns.

Unfortunately, Palmer's second season at Hillsborough did not end in glory as the Owls were relegated.

His third season was so much better for him and anybody connected to Hillsborough. He only missed two games that season, playing 57 times, and was one of the main reasons Wednesday gained promotion and reached the Wembley League Cup final. One of the saddest things about Carlton's career at Sheffield Wednesday was the fact that he had to miss the League Cup Final victory over Manchester United.

The following season, 1991-1992, he played every game in the top division when Wednesday gained a very respectable top seven position. In one of those games, against Queens Park Rangers, he even managed to score a first half hat trick.

It was that same season that Palmer won the first of his 18 full England international caps against, Russia.

I think only three English players have bettered that total whilst playing for the Sheffield Wednesday Football Club: Ron Springett, Ernest Blenkinsop and Peter Swan. He played for his country in the European Championships and was one of the few successes in their rather disappointing efforts.

Palmer was a talkative lad during the game and always had something to say, generally, pointedly, to the opposition. Many a referee has pulled out the yellow card as a way of trying to quell his verbal over exuberance. He would never be put off his stride and always played the same way. It sometimes cost him dear in bookings, fined and missed games, but it was the only style he knew and he never wavered from giving the fans his total commitment, every game.

Carlton never seemed to get the recognition his play deserved, the supporters of Sheffield Wednesday always found Carlton Palmer a solid, energetic midfielder who could give excellent cover for full back or centre half duties and he was never afraid to 'get stuck in'. But even his England appearances were derided by some snipers saying he was selected by Graham Taylor, who many football pundits have ridiculed.

I personally think for a period of time in the early 1990s Carlton Palmer was as good a midfielder as there was in the English Football League.

Carlton played over 250 games for Sheffield Wednesday and scored 18 goals, 7 of them in his last season. He went the way of a large amount of the Owls players in the early 1990s, to Howard Wilkinson's Leeds United.

Wilkinson had won the Championship the season before with a large array of ex Wednesday talent: Chapman, Sterland, Shutt, Snodin, Cantona (a little cheeky that one) and now he was taking Palmer, for £2.6 million.

Caarlton Palmer (Sheff Wed & England)

Palmer played 130 games for Leeds United and was then sold to Southampton, after 52 apperances he moved on to Nottingham Forest, only stayed for 16 games and then moved to Coventry where he played just 35 times. Some time later he was loaned back to Sheffield Wednesday when they found themselves in trouble near the foot of the division. Carlton played in over 700 league games and scored 40 goals in a career that had three transfers of over one million pounds.

In November 2001 he tried management at Stockport County but did not fair too well as the club were already on the slide and Palmer could do little to halt the inevitable.

Wednesday

John **Sheridan**

John Sheridan was 25 years old when he joined Sheffield Wednesday from Nottingham Forest. He had already played over 260 first team games for Leeds and had been through the trauma of a broken leg, just after his 19th birthday, when playing against Barnsley. John made a full recovery from this early setback in his career to come back the following season and be an ever present team member.

In 1988 Sheridan, now 24 years old, was in such good form for Leeds that astute former Wednesday manager Jack Charlton, now the Irish coach, picked John to represent his country. John was selected through parental qualification to play against Rumania and so gained the first of his 34 international caps, 29 of those caps were gained whilst John was a Wednesday player. He also played in two World Cups with the Irish team.

Sheridan was transferred to Nottingham Forest for £650,000 and never appeared in a league game for them. His only appearance under Brian Clough was in one league cup game. The Wednesday manager at the time, Ron Atkinson, kept an eye on what was happening at Forest and stepped in to buy John for a reduced price of £500,000. Three months at Cloughie's Forest was enough for Sheridan. He formed a grand midfield at Hillsborough along with Carlton Palmer and Danny Wilson, but his first season ended with Wednesday losing five of their last six games and being relegated.

The next season, 1990-91, was Sheridan's most productive season for Wednesday, he scored 12 goals and played in every game bar one. Wednesday gained promotion back to the top flight and had a good run in the FA cup and went on to win the League Cup with a Wembley victory against Manchester United, 1-0. Sheridan's only League cup goal of that season was the spectacular little beauty he whacked past Les Sealey in the Manchester goal. Now that one did bring a tear to the eye.

June 1995, when John was still only 30 years old, was a very telling time for the Owls fans. David Pleat was selected to be the new manager, he was not a Sheridan fan and so a career that still had a place at Hillsborough was ended too early by a manager who brought in Scott Oakes to replace him.

John went on loan to Birmingham City and Bolton Wanderers before he finally joined the latter for £200,000 during the 1996-97 campaign.

Sheridan was a player with great awareness of the position of players around him. He could play the ball long with accuracy directly to the awaiting players feet, he was brilliant at free kicks and was very rarely caught in possession. Sheridan was one of only two players I have seen grace Hillsborough who had the talent to find space. Not just to run into empty parts of the pitch but right in the middle of the hurly burly of a top flight game he seemed to be shouting for the ball. When he received it, he always had enough time to control it, look up and invariably make a telling pass without any opposition player getting near him. A very talented midfield player who through poor managerial decisions was released too early.

John Sheridan (Sheff Wed & Eire)

Sheridan himself stated that after the loss of the cup finals in 1993 he thinks the club got rid of some players too soon. This, I imagine, helped to start the slide in fortune which did not stop for nearly a decade. John saw the departure of Ron Atkinson as the reason the Owls did not follow the 1991 League Cup triumph with more silverware. Sheridan stated that if Atkinson had stayed another three or four seasons, the Owls would definitely have won more major honours.

Sheridan played 242 league and cup games for the Owls and scored on 33 occasions.

Roland **Nilsson**

Swedish international full back, Roland Nilsson, came to Sheffield Wednesday from IFK Gothenburg in late 1989 for a fee of £375,000. He was bought as a replacement for ex club captain, Mel Sterland, who had departed for Glasgow Rangers after a dispute with the manager, Peter Eustace.

Ron Atkinson, the new manager at Hillsborough, talked Nilsson into coming to Sheffield Wednesday in preference to going to Manchester United. Roland played for the last 20 games of season 1989-90 but could not help to make up the points, which Wednesday had dropped after a truly dreadful start to the campaign. They only gained one win out of their first 11 games played and only managed another 10 wins all season. So in Roland's first few month in England his new team, Sheffield Wednesday, were relegated. He must have been thinking about that offer from Manchester United!

Redfern Froggatt (Sheff Wed & England)

In fairness to Roland, and all the other players they stayed at Hillsborough and put their best efforts in to getting the team back into the top division. This was something I think the fans really appreciated. No holding the club to clauses written into their contracts, "if the team is relegated I can be allowed to leave". Which I have heard a couple of them had.

The next season was vastly different and it was not until the 15th game of the season that Wednesday had a setback. It was actually a double setback, as the Owls lost to Millwall at the Den and Nilsson himself was injured and missed the next 20 games. Nilsson did not get back to fitness until April when Wednesday had reached the final of the League (Rumbelows) Cup and had almost clinched promotion.

I think Roland may well have let his recuperation take a little longer if Wednesday had not been up for the two honours, promotion and a Wembley appearance in the league cup final.

He was deemed fit enough, by manager Atkinson, and played in the final, with a little help from John Harkes, and appeared in the last seven league games of the season, sharing in the glory of that fine April and May.

Roland was an integral part of the team that took Wednesday to four Wembley appearances in 1993, finished 3rd in the top division, played in European club football, and managed 7th position in seasons 1992-93 and 1993-94. Sadly for Sheffield Wednesday Roland Nilsson left the club for personal reasons in May 1994.

He played 184 games for Sheffield Wednesday before returning to Sweden where he played for Helsingborg for three years. In 1997 Ron Atkinson persuaded him to come back to England and play for Coventry City. Nilsson spent two seasons at Highfield Road in which he performed outstandingly in the Coventry defence and was one of the main reasons the Sky Blues remained in the top flight.

He returned to Sweden once more for another spell with Helsingborg, eventually becoming coach of the side, Nilsson was invited back to Coventry by Gordon Strachan and returned to Highfield Road in 2001 to work alongside his former team-mate as a coach. Following Coventry's relegation to the First Division and a poor start to the 2001/2002 season, Strachan left the club and Nilsson took over as manager. This only lasted one season before Roland was dismissed.

Nilsson had a fine international career with his country, Sweden, gaining 112 caps. He played in two World Cup final stages, 1990, 1994, and reached a semi-final. He also played in International European Championships, once again reaching a semi-final.

Wednesday

Danny **Wilson**

At the start of the 1990-1991 season Sheffield Wednesday bought a 30 year old midfielder who I had seen many times plying his trade with Luton, amongst other clubs and had already played in over 500 league and cup games. A player who through his skill, grit, determination and energy level was an instant hit with the Owls fans. Danny Wilson came in to a good, but relegated, side in August 1990 and for the next nine months played a vital part in what was, possibly, the most lucrative season in Sheffield Wednesday's history, culminating with a winning trip to Wembley, and promotion back up into the top division.

Wilson, a Northern Ireland international, made 125 starting appearances for the Owls and scored 14 goals, seven of them in that 1991 cup winning season. Danny played for three full seasons and appeared at Wembley on three occasions, (missing the first FA Cup final), gained promotion and finished in the top 8 in both his seasons in the top flight.

Danny Wilson (Sheff Wed & N Ireland)

Wilson was somewhat of a regular at Wembley. He had won the Littlewoods Cup (League Cup) in 1988 and lost in the final of same competition the following year 1989. So in four years Danny had made three League Cup final appearances, two of them successful.

I was a fan of Danny Wilson long before he ever played for Sheffield Wednesday, and I think he was one of Ron Atkinson's more astute signings. A player who had a great engine, he never stopped running, he was a brilliant foil for Sheridan's less energetic, but brilliant style of play. Along with Sheridan and Carlton Palmer, I personally thought that it was as good a midfield as the Owls have had for many years.

Wilson was a communicator on the pitch, he always seemed to be directing the situation, be it at the back or at set plays, he always had a say. He was a player who you would see taking or looking for an opportunity in the opposition's penalty area one minute and the next be clearing off of his own goal line or helping out with defensive duties. For a man whose Sheffield Wednesday career started after his 30th birthday he seemed to be as fit or fitter that almost everyone, possibly with the exception of Carlton Palmer.

Danny Wilson's last game for Sheffield Wednesday was in the 1993 FA Cup Final replay in front of almost seventy thousand fans at Wembley. This game, which we sadly lost 2-1, was only the second ever match, at Wembley, to have the start delayed – 1923, the White Horse final, being the other.

Wilson's record whilst a Wednesday player speaks for itself. He played 136 games (including substitution appearances). He won 67, drew 43 and lost only 26 games. This success rate of 65% is amongst the best of any player who has played for the Owls in my era of visiting Hillsborough.

After his departure from Sheffield Wednesday he was appointed to assistant manager at Barnsley and soon moved into the Manager's chair. In 1996-97, along with his old team mate, Peter Shirtliff, who was player coach, he achieved the phenomenal feat of getting Barnsley into the now money laden premiership. It only lasted a season (possibly as good as Barnsley could have expected) but it raised Wilson's status in the managerial market and he was soon tempted back to Sheffield Wednesday to fill his old manager's, Ron Atkinson, boots.

It became a sad situation of a Sheffield Wednesday hero coming back to manage his old club with high expectation. However, as usual the bitter taste of failure prevailed. In Danny's defence the two Italian players, Carbone and Di Canio, spoiled the time he was in charge with their regular tantrums and indiscipline. It made it an almost impossible position for Wilson. He was caught between the crowd's love of two skillful, but unruly, players and a manager's duty to do what was right for the club.

John **Harkes**

John Harkes came to Sheffield Wednesday from United States Soccer after being spotted playing for the University of North Carolina. He was a great buy for the Owls at £70,000 in 1990, an era when transfers of some three million pound were being paid. He came to Hillsborough as the current United States of America international team captain where he was generally used as a midfielder. Ron Atkinson played him, on his first team debut, at right back in place of the injured Roland Nilsson. So in November 1990 at Hillsborough versus Oldham, in the second division, John Harkes started his eventful and lucrative stay at Sheffield Wednesday Football Club.

Before I detail Johns' grand efforts with the Owls his portfolio of other accomplishments is staggering: Various player of year awards for US High School, Colleges etc; He was a 1988 US Olympic team member; National player of the year; gained 90 caps over an eleven year period; captained his various schools, colleges, University as well as D.C. United and the US team; played in two World Cups; voted Most Valuable player in 1995 Copa America; selected in 1996 World All Stars; MLS Cup Championship Winner, twice; InterAmerican Cup Championship Winner and US Open Cup Championship Winner.

His résumé in England does not read too badly either: League Cup Winners Medal 1991; League Cup Runners-up medal, in 1993, when we lost 1-2 to Arsenal. In this game he became the first American to score in an English Cup Final when he knocked the ball past David Seaman after only nine minutes; FA Cup Final runners-up medal, also in 1993, when we drew 1-1 with Arsenal and lost 1-2 in the replay (I think I dislike Arsenal more than Everton). Scorer of Goal of the Season 1993 (against his future club, Derby); John was also one of the most successful players on Wednesday records. In his three seasons as a player with the Owls he played in 114 games and was only on the losing side on 24 occasions.

Harkes turned out in numerous positions for the Owls but was mainly used in midfield by Atkinson and Francis. His abilities were: to cover ground, never (it seemed) stop running, excellent tackling and skill on the ball. He was liked by the crowd and was popular with all his team mates. It seemed to indicate John would be at Hillsborough for a long stay. Football never seems to work like that, does it?

After a good season and four Wembley appearances it seemed like the only position that needed strengthening was goalkeeper, or at least let Pressman play. However, in August 1993, Trevor Francis sold Harkes to Derby County for a fee of £850,000. A nice profit of three quarters of a million was made but I am not sure it was a good move to lose a player of his class. Andy Sinton from QPR (Francis's old club) was brought in to replace Harkes. I, personally, don't think he ever did.

John Harkes (Sheff Wed & U.S.A.)

The transfer from Wednesday to Derby County made John Harkes the first American soccer player to be sold for over one million dollars. The Derby fans took to John Harkes much the same way as the Owls supporters did and he was there for two season until the USA Soccer Federation bought him back for around half a million pound. He was later loaned back to English Football where West Ham United took him on. He made his debut for the Hammers at Hillsborough when they defeated Wednesday 1-0. Old boy comes back to haunt Owls – that's a headline we've seen a time or two.

In John Harkes's biography "Captain for Life" he is described by Bruce Arena, the USA football coach, "as the most accomplished player in the history of U.S. soccer".

Wednesday

Paul **Warhurst**

Paul Warhurst was perceived as one of the most promising youngsters in the game during the late 1980s. Strangely he had been released by Manchester City who sold him to Oldham Athletic. Warhurst was a regular at the centre of the Oldham defence and played all along the back line. He was capped at England Under 21 level several times playing at right back.

He was an integral part of the defence in the successful cup runs which Oldham had during the late 1980s. They also gained promotion along with Sheffield Wednesday in 1991.

Paul Warhurst (Sheffield Wednesday)

In 1991, Trevor Francis was put in charge at Hillsborough. After the untimely departure of Ron Atkinson to Aston Villa, he decided to break up the Cup Winning side and rebuild a new team.

Paul Warhurst was Trevor Francis's first buy, a snip at £750,000. The crowd seemed to take to him in those early games but after a few mistakes in defence he was in and out of the first team and appeared on the substitutes bench more and more regularly.

It was in his following season, 1992-1993, that Francis tried Warhurst up front when Hirst was injured. A positional switch that seemed to be a managerial masterstroke. Warhurst played alongside Mark Bright and surprised all the fans, and possibly himself, by scoring a stunning haul of 17 goals, six in the league and 11 in the cup games. Some of the goals Paul Warhurst scored were exceptionally high quality. He popped in headed goals, one or two from distance, poachers goals, and two little gems in the Blackburn semi-final. The one I recall as the best he scored was against Derby County when he was put through by a chip from John Sheridan and he had to be at full stretch to knock it in the net on the volley. The speed and timing of the run by Warhurst and the pass by Sheridan epitomised Sheffield Wednesday in that early part of 1993.

When it all clicked, no team in the country could live with the Owls; Sheridan and Waddle supplying inch perfect passes to the forwards; Palmer, Hyde and Harkes winning the ball in midfield; Pearson, Anderson, Nilsson and Shirtliff so solid in defence and Bright and Warhurst with help from Hirst and Watson banging in the goals. During the early months of 1993 Paul Warhurst equalled Derek Dooley's 40 year old record of scoring in seven consecutive matches, he was on fire in front of goal and would have a shot from anywhere. In the League Cup semi final he scored two goals and in the FA Cup semi final, against Sheffield United, he hit the woodwork twice, both from from distance. He was showing such excellent scoring form he was selected to join the England squad.

Strangely, it was the injuries to the two central defenders that seemed to be the undoing of Sheffield Wednesday that season. With Pearson breaking a leg in the semi final with Blackburn and Shirtliff also suffering two separate injuries it was deemed Warhurst and Carlton Palmer should be pulled back into defence for the latter part of the season. Hirst was almost fit again and so we went into the two cup finals against Arsenal with almost a new team formation.

The two losses in the Cup finals, the FA Cup after a replay, were hard to take. I think a few of the senior players left Trevor Francis in no doubt as to their feelings on team selection. Players were reported, in the newspapers, to have said this and said that and Paul Warhurst was supposedly very unhappy at being asked to move into the back four. I really don't think Francis had much option, but it did seem to cause a little friction within the club at a time when, you would imagine, unity would be paramount.

Those games were the last Warhurst played for Wednesday, he moved on to Blackburn Rovers for a fee in excess of £2.5 million in August 1993 just three months after making four Wembley appearances for the Owls.

Paul did not have the best of luck at Blackburn, breaking both legs in his first year. He did not really succeed at Ewood Park and soon moved on to Bolton Wanderers where he stayed for a few years.

A young man who when playing up front for the Owls, for that six month period, looked as good a player as I have seen in that position since David Layne in the 1960s.

Paul Warhurst, was a versatile young player, who after playing 80 games in just over two seasons was allowed to leave Hillsborough far too early.

Wednesday

Chris **Waddle**

Chris Waddle (Sheff Wed & England)

Chris Waddle was one of the best, if not the best, signings Sheffield Wednesday have ever made.

A Geordie, who played his early football with Tow Law Town, before being snapped up by Newcastle United in 1980, was to become a Newcastle legend in his 6 years at St James Park. He scored 52 goals in 190 games for Newcastle United.

Surprisingly he was allowed to leave and headed south to Tottenham Hotspur for a fee in excess of £500,000. He played for Spurs for four seasons and reached an FA Cup final losing to Coventry City 3-2. One fact I did find surprising is that Chris Waddle was top scorer at White Hart Lane in one of his seasons there - brilliant winger, superb crosser and dead ball expert - but leading scorer?

When Spurs developed financial problems, as even the big clubs do, they decided to sell Waddle to Marseilles for a record fee of £4.25 million, making a vast profit but losing a brilliant player.

He had three years at the French Club, winning the League title in his first season and retaining it for the remainder of his time in France. He reached a European Champions Cup final losing to Red Star Belgrade.

When Trevor Francis signed Waddle in 1992, for a £1 million fee, it did look another piece of good football management by a man who could coax the better players to Sheffield 6.

Chris Waddle, after a couple of niggling little injuries, was to show in his first season that class really does count.

He seemed to be able to beat his man at will, no knocking the ball up the wing and chasing after it, he would coax the defender into a lunge or just by moving his feet, not the ball, he could create space for an accurate cross. He delighted the fans with his skillful wing play and helped Sheffield Wednesday to a League Cup Final and also the FA Cup final.

On the way to the FA Cup final the Owls had to play Sheffield United at Wembley in the 'Steel City' semi-final. In the first few minutes a free kick was awarded against the United defence, up stepped Waddle to lash in a thunderous shot from all of 30 yards. Alan Kelly, one of the best keepers in the country, at that time, was nowhere near it.

Waddle also scored in the Cup Final replay against Arsenal a couple of weeks later.

At the end of that brilliant but disappointing season Waddle's only trophy was a personal one; The Football Writers Association Player of the Year, for 1992-1993, a trophy no other Wednesday player has won, before or since.

Chris played for another three years for the Owls, not as exciting as the first season but intermittently the football was still brilliant to watch.

With the dismissal of Trevor Francis and the appointment of David Pleat, I think Waddle knew his days at Hillsborough were numbered. The crowed wanted Waddle to become assistant manager to Pleat, but I think 'Old David' had other plans.

Chris Waddle was allowed to leave Sheffield Wednesday in the 1996-1997 season when he went to Bradford City where he was an immediate hit with the fans. He also had a period playing for Sunderland. He tried management with Burnley, but that was not the success he would have hoped for. He has applied for the managers job at Hillsborough, on several occasions, well it does go up for offer quite regularly.

Chris still lives in Sheffield and turns out for a local football club on Sundays. A footballer who carries on playing just for the enjoyment of the game.

A wonderful player who is up there amongst the best players who have ever pulled on the blue and white stripes of Sheffield Wednesday.

Wednesday

Des **Walker**

Hackney born Des Walker started his professional football career at Brian Clough's Nottingham Forest in March 1984. Within five years he was being described as the most reliable central defender in the country. Bobby Robson agreed with this assessment and selected Des to make his England debut in 1988-89 season. Within 18 months Des was to become an automatic choice for England. In the 1990 World Cup, where England reached the semi-final, he was voted the tournament's outstanding player. Des played 57 times for England. In his eight year career at Nottingham Forest, Des Walker helped his team win two League Cup finals, reach an FA Cup final, losing to Spurs when he unfortunately scored the winning goal for Spurs with a perfectly placed header past his own keeper. Forest also finished third in the top division in two of Des Walker's nine season at the City ground.

At the end of the 1992 season Des, now at the end of his contract, exercised his option to leave Nottingham Forest for a pre-determined fee of £1.5 million. The fee did not really match the player's true market value which would have been around £3-4 million if he had not been out of contract. Walker signed for Sampdoria and, unfortunately, was never the great success he was expected to be. In fact Des only played one full season in Italy and was grateful for Trevor Francis's interest in bringing him back to England and Sheffield Wednesday for a fee in excess of £2.75 million – a Wednesday record.

So on 14th August 1993 Des Walker played his first league game for the Owls and went on to complete a full season of 42 league games, four FA cup appearances and eight League Cup appearances. I would imagine you could count the number of mistakes Des made in that first season on one hand. He fitted in as though he had played with the Owls players for years. It was an excellent debut season, and one in which he was voted Sheffield Wednesday player of season.

Over the next seven seasons Des Walker was without doubt the most consistent player at Hillsborough.

Des must have thought that he was coming back from Italy into one of the top English sides after seeing Wednesday's results and cup runs for the previous three years, but in all honesty he came back into a side which Trevor Francis was breaking up and trying to rebuild. I think Des Walker was seen as the rock which Francis would build a new team around.

Unfortunately, it did not work out that way. This is not to say Wednesday were a spent force, far from it. They had good cup runs and finished well placed in the Premiership in Walker's first few seasons. Possibly, given time, Francis may well have been able to deliver his new team. But time and football management are not easy bedfellows.

Francis's teambuilding, unfortunately, did not deliver results quickly enough and he was soon replaced by David Pleat.

If Pleat had purchased players with the determination and enthusiasm of Des perhaps things would have worked out. It did seem at the time of the slide out of the Premiership that some of our more costly purchases never really had the heart for a fight, in fact a good number spent a lot more time on the injury table than on the field of play.

Des Walker (Sheff Wed & England)

The lack of consistency during Wednesday's slump was possibly because Des Walker never really had a defensive partner who played alongside him for any period of time. Newsome, Stefanovic, Pearce, Watts, Atherton, Coleman, Ingersson plus a few more were all willing players but none were really up to the task of making it a long term partnership to combat the premiership strikeforces.

In 2001 Walker refused a reduced contract at Sheffield Wednesday and went into the football wilderness for a few months until his old club Forest put him back on their payroll.

In a career spanning 20 full seasons Des played 307 games for Wednesday and 320 for Forest, plus 30 games in Italy. With his international appearances this gives him over 700 games played nearly all at the top level of English, Italian and International football. He scored his one and only goal during his first spell at Nottingham Forest in the 1991-92 season.

A great servant to Wednesday and football in general.

Wednesday

Benito **Carbone**

Before he was transferred to Sheffield Wednesday in 1996, Benito Carbone had played over 150 games in Italy. He started his professional football career at Torino, moved to Ascoli, Reggina, Casertana, Torino again, Napoli and finally Inter Milan in 1995. Within this six years of whirlwind transfers and loans he managed 24 goals.

Benito Carbone (Sheffield Wednesday)

His best season of goalscoring was six for Ascoli in 1992-1993.

Carbone was a breath of fresh air when he arrived at Hillsborough for a £3 million fee. He had an ability to go past a man, spray passes to all parts of the pitch, invariably to a team mate, and for such a slight character have a pop at goal from some unbelievable distances. He seemed to be a player who was destined to be up there with the best we had ever seen.

In this first season at Hillsborough, 1996-1997, he played in 24 games and scored 6 goals. Not a bad return when playing with a new side. He looked to be the ideal midfielder. He made chance after chance for his team mates and was always willing to have a go, from almost anywhere inside the opposition's half.

The little Italian loved the adulation and lifted his game accordingly. When interviewed after the match by television or radio you could see that he relished the responsibility that was being heaped upon him by David Pleat. He was the man in midfield who made it all tick for the 1996-97 season.

He continued much in the same vein in the following season, but David Pleat seemed to waste all the pre season trying to tempt Paolo Di Canio from Celtic to play alongside

Carbone and did seem to neglect some of the other areas that needed strengthening.

Benito Carbone still showed his magic and proceeded to score nine goals in each of his next two seasons when he played 33 games in 1997-98 and 31 games in 1998-1999. This was a very respectable goalscoring return for any midfielder. Unfortunately for Carbone he was no longer the centre of attention at Hillsborough, Di Canio was on the scene now and as he had done at Celtic, almost demanded centre stage. I saw interviews on television where the pair were being interviewed and questions directly asked of Carbone were answered by Di Canio. Paolo seemed to dominate, not only his countryman but Sheffield Wednesday themselves.

It all came to a sad ending in the 1999-2000 season when Carbone refused Danny Wilson's instructions to take his place on the substitutes bench in a game at Southampton. He left the stadium and, I am led to believe, departed for Italy. This was the end for the little Italian. He was loaned out to Aston Villa, where he played 24 games. He only played another seven games for the Owls, scoring 2 goals in the 1999-2000 season.

I personally thought he might regain some of his old stature after the disappointing departure of the overbearing Di Canio, but it was not to be and with his regular disputes with Danny Wilson it was not long before he was loaned out and then sold on for a ridiculous knockdown fee.

Carbone was a player who was without doubt blessed with God given football talent but it somehow never developed into the trophies or international caps it really deserved. Wednesday, Aston Villa, Derby County, Bradford City, Middlesborough all played Carbone and all thought, initially, he was just the man they had been looking for – but sadly in all cases it proved not to be the case.

The last I heard about Benito he was playing for Como and then Parma back in Italy. What could have been Benni?

Paolo **Di Canio**

Paolo Di Canio was 29 years old when he came to Sheffield Wednesday from Scottish club Celtic, in 1997. He had already played for six clubs, Lazio, Ternana, Lazio again, Juventus, Napoli, AC Milan and Celtic.

This, much travelled, midfielder cum striker arrived at Hillsborough after what seemed an amazingly long transfer wrangle with Celtic. They did not want him to leave but Paolo, being the person he is, wanted away. So at the start of 1997-1998 season we saw the Di Canio Roadshow hit town, with all its baggage.

Before knowing anything about Di Canio's temperament, we all settled down for a season and watched a master in the art of football. He made fools of the best defenders in the country. There wasn't a defender who, man to man, could contain him, his footwork was amazing. His bag of tricks contained some glorious stuff, flicks, overhead kicks, long or short passes, neat little one two's, especially with Carbone, free kicks, and best of all, 14 wonderful goals.

His infectious personality and determination to make those around him perform, made him a favourite with the supporters within a couple of games of his debut. Along with the other Italian, Benito Carbone, we had an attacking format that looked for all the world like it could bring back the good times of a couple of years earlier. They gelled, not only as team mates but also as friends and were always seen together not only at Hillsborough but around the Sheffield area.

Paolo's temperament sometimes left a little to be desired but we could live with that. After all he was our temperamental player, so a little show of Italian hotheadedness didn't matter too much, did it?

David Pleat who purchased Di Canio for Sheffield Wednesday was not finding good results easy to come by and once again the powers that be at Hillsborough decided it was time for a change.

Ex Wednesday player Danny Wilson was brought in, as manager, from Barnsley. This caused a little acrimony between the clubs, but Danny knew it was a step up the managerial ladder, so a well liked ex-player came back as boss.

I don't think Wilson really liked the two Italian's lack of discipline and within a couple of months of the start of the 1998-1999 season he was to be proved correct. Five league games into the year, on 26th September 1998 against Arsenal, Di Canio let his temper boil over. Referee Alcock gave a decision that Paolo did not agree with. The foul by Keown, wasn't on Di Canio himself, but being the type of player who orchestrates everything his team does he stormed in and tried to sort the matter out. A scuffle ensued, punches were thrown, and Di Canio and Keown were sent from the field of play. This decision did not go down too well with the players

Paolo Di Canio (Sheffield Wednesday)

or the crowd and Di Canio seemed to lose any control he had and pushed the referee over. I do think the ref made a meal of it. But in football you are not allowed to lay a hand on the referee, a rule that really must be upheld.

This was the beginning of the end for Paolo at Hillsborough, he was banned for months and was subsequently released to West Ham United for an unbelievable low fee of only £1.5 million.

The seasons since his departure are testament of what could have been at Hillsborough. He will always be hotheaded but with someone who cajoles him, like Harry Redknapp, you can have your cake and eat it. A wonderfully annoying player.

Wednesday

Wednesday players who nearly made the list

Peter Johnson alias Charlie, played for the Owls for eight seasons. He was purchased from Rotherham United in December 1957 and after a couple of seasons settling in he became a regular from 1959 onwards.

Peter Johnson (Sheffield Wednesday)

He was an ever present in the 1960-61 season when we finished second to the double winning Spurs side. He was quick, defensively reliable and chipped in with the odd goal. The left wingers of the day found it a difficult task to get any joy when playing against Johnson. He never seemed to dive in with a reckless challenge he always seemed to either make them pass backwards or relieve them of the ball. Ron Springett, the Owls keeper, did not have to deal with too many crosses from the opposition left wingers.

Right full back, Johnson and left back Don Megson were a strong defensive partnership for five full seasons until Peter lost his first team place to Brian Hill in 1964. He was transferred to Peterborough United by Alan Brown.

Roy Shiner was born on the Isle of Wight in 1924 and came to Hillsborough from Huddersfield in 1955. To sign a player over 30 years old seemed a risky thing to do but Eric Taylor took the gamble and it certainly paid off. In his four full seasons with Wednesday he notched 96 goals in 160 appearances.

Roy Shiner (Sheffield Wednesday)

He scored 33 goals in his first season with Wednesday and also claimed a second division championship medal. He scored 16 goals in each of his next two seasons, both in Division One, the latter season saw the Owls relegated.

Season 1958-1959 was another Second Division championship medal and Roy was back to his best with 28 goals in 38 games. His final season was 1959-1960 when he only managed nine games, scoring three times before Harry Catterick sold him to Hull City, at the age of 35.

Andrew Wilson came from Glasgow Clyde in 1900 and stayed with Wednesday for 20 years. He scored 216 goals and played in 545 games. He was a Scottish International with six full caps to his name and he was top goalscorer with Wednesday in eight out of his 16 seasons.

Andrew Wilson (Sheff Wed and Scotland)

He played in the League Championship winning sides of 1903 and 1904 as well as gaining an FA Cup Winners medal in 1907. His record is slightly better that stated, because he played some wartime games, which do not count in official records, but he did play another 75 games and scored 25 goals for the Wednesday.

Andrew Wilson played only one league game for the Owls after the end of the First World War and then decided to go into management where he was in charge at Bristol Rovers, Oldham Athletic and Stockport County.

Jackie Sewell signed for Sheffield Wednesday for a British record fee of £35,000 in 1951 and in his 175 appearances for the Owls, over five season, he notched over a goal every two games scoring on 92 occasions.

Jackie Sewell (Sheff Wed and England)

During his stay at Hillsborough Jackie gained six England caps, one of them being against Hungary in 1953 when England suffered a shock defeat at Wembley by the visitors. Sewell also gained other representative honours playing for the English League against the League of Ireland, in 1954, at Maine Road, where he scored a fine hat-trick. Weeks later he was back at the same ground to play in a FA Cup semi-final for Wednesday against Preston North End, sadly losing 2-0 to the Lancashire side. Jackie was transferred to Aston Villa in 1955, and two years later played at Wembley and won the FA Cup for them. He was later transferred to Hull City.

Gary Shelton came from Aston Villa in a deal worth £50,000 (a steal) in the latter part of season 1981-1982. He made an immediate contribution to the side and within two years Wednesday were in the first division. In the Owls promotion year Shelton weighed in with seven goals, one of them the only goal of the game away at Newcastle to complete a marvellous double over the Geordies.

Now in the top flight Shelton did not look out of place and after only eight games he had scored three times, the one that gave most pleasure was the goal he knocked in at Liverpool to give Wednesday a famous away victory.

Gary Shelton (Sheffield Wednesday)

Shelton was born in Nottingham and made his football league debut with Walsall when only 16. He went on to play for Aston Villa before his move to the Owls, where he stayed for just over five years managing 239 games and scoring 24 goals. Gary moved on in 1987 to Oxford and later to Bristol City, where they won their league and finally to Chester as player-coach. Gary played in over 600 games for all his six clubs.

Vic Mobley came from Oxford City in September 1961. He was bought to be the understudy to Peter Swan, who was then the incumbent England centre half. Swan's career was cut short by the bribes scandal so Mobley was drafted in and never really looked back. He was a big built, blonde, lad who could out muscle most of the centre forwards of the day and also knocked in the odd goal.

On the back of the bribes case Wednesday needed someone to help us through and this young man was up to the job. He played every game in 1964-65 when the Owls finished a very respectable 8th. Season 1965-1966 saw Mobley dogged by two different injuries. He was selected to play for England, at centre half, but sustained an injury the week before the international and was never selected again. His second injury, that season, came in the semi-final game at Villa Park against Chelsea. In days when no subs were allowed, Mobley injured on the half hour, bravely battled on for another 60 minutes, he also made Graham Pugh's goal. The injury deemed he missed the final. Mobley played 210 games for Wednesday before leaving for QPR in 1969 for £55,000.

Vic Mobley (Sheffield Wednesday)

Johnny Quinn joined Wednesday from Prescott Cables in 1959 initially as an inside forward.

Over the next nine seasons Quinn would play in almost every position except goal for the Owls. He was Mr Versatile, play anywhere, never seemed to moan about his lot and invariably turned in a good, solid, performance.

1964-1965 was John's best season. New manager Alan Brown liked Quinny and he played him at inside right. John responded to this with a series of excellent displays and seven goals, one of them, the only goal of the game, against Liverpool.

John Quinn (Sheffield Wednesday)

Quinn played against Everton in the 1966 cup final and remained at Hillsborough for another two seasons before he was transferred to Rotherham United. Arguably, John played his best football at Millmoor. Tommy Doherty, the Miller's manager, made Quinn captain and played him at wing half where his skills blossomed even more. John played 195 games for the Owls and 114 games for Rotherham before moving on to Halifax Town.

Phil King was born in Bristol and played his first football league games with local sides Exeter City and Torquay United. He was transferred to Swindon Town in 1987 where he gained promotion and was receiving rave notices for his solid performances.

Sheffield Wednesday moved in for him in season 1989-90. He made 25 league appearances but unfortunately the Owls were relegated. He played in all but three games the next season, when Wednesday won promotion back to the top flight and also won the League Cup against, high flying, Manchester United.

Phil King was a reliable full back whose partnership with Roland Nilsson was one of the main reasons Wednesday were so solid at the back. After promotion back to the top division he only missed four games and Wednesday finished in third place, their highest placing for over 30 years.

Phil King (Sheffield Wednesday)

Phil suffered a cruciate ligament injury in 1992 and struggled to regain his place in the Owls side. He move to Aston Villa for £250,000, but sadly suffered another cruciate ligament injury in November 1995.

Dan Petrescu was transferred to Hillsborough from Italian club Genoa for a fee in excess of £1,2500 in June 1994.

Trevor Francis, obviously, saw Petrescu as a quality player who could fit in down the right side of the Sheffied Wednesday defence

or midfield. Unfortunately, Trevor did not last that long at Hillsborough after he bought Petrescu, and in came David Pleat. Pleat did not seem to rate the Rumanian that highly and he was only playing in the first team intermittently. The more progressive people at Chelsea were monitoring the situation and arrived with a £2,300,000 offer that Wednesday did not refuse.

Dan Petrescu was a class act, something he never had the chance to show at Hillsborough. Petrescu was an automatic choice for his country, scoring a winning goal against England in the World Cup and showed his excellent midfield attacking talents for Chelsea, where he won a FA cup medal and was a

Dan Petrescu (Sheff Wed & Romania)

great crowd pleaser.

After only 41 league and cup games Wednesday sold a player who could have been an great assett for five or six more seasons.

Mark Bright came from Crystal Palace in late 1992 for over £1million cash plus Paul Williams. A large sum of money for a player who was already 30 years old.

Bright partnered Ian Wright in the Palace side that did so well in the late 1980s and early 1990s, both scoring prolifically. When Wright joined Arsenal in late1991, Bright still knocked 20 goals in as the lone striker. Wednesday moved in for him in early August 1992.

In his first season with Wednesday he scored 20 goals and appeared in a League Cup final and a FA Cup final which needed a replay. Sadly both finals were lost. His second season was more prolific, he notched 23 league and cup goals and the Owls finished,

Mark Bright (Sheffield Wednesday)

respectably, in 7th spot. Mark who left Hillsborough for Charlton Athletic is now retired and works for TV as a soccer pundit.

Jim McCalliog was a Glasgow born lad who seemed to be set for a brilliant career with Chelsea. He was knocking in goals at every level he played at. For some reason the London club sold him to Wednesday in October 1965 for a then record fee for a teenager of £37,500. He would come back to haunt his old club.

It was not a great first season, for Jim, at Hillsborough and

Wednesday only managed 14 wins out of a possible 42 games played. Finishing way down in 17th place in the league the Owls faired much better in the FA Cup. On the way to the final, Sheffield Wednesday played McCalliog's old club Chelsea at Villa Park, inevitably he scored the second goal and Wednesday won 2-0 and booked a place at Wembley. Jim also scored in the final, but the outcome was different.

Playing 174 games and scoring 27 goals, Jim never really lived up to the expectations we all thought were possible after his first year. He moved on to play for Wolves, Manchester United and Southampton where he won a FA

Jim McCalliog (Sheff Wed & Scotland)

Cup winner medal. He was capped 5 times by Scotland whilst playing for Sheffield Wednesday. A skillful little player.

Brian Hornsby was one of Jack Charlton's first signings in 1978, when he was bought from Shrewsbury Town, where he had played for two years. Brian started his career at Arsenal after he had been spotted playing schoolboy and youth international level for England. He made 33 appearances for the Gunners.

After his arrival in March 1978, Hornsby played the last 13 games of that season and followed it up with a memorable 1978-1979 season where he proceeded to score 21 league and cup goals from a midfield position.

That season Hornsby played in nine FA cup ties, now most players don't play that many cup games in two or three season, never mind in a 5 month period. It was due, of course, to the marathon tie, of 5 games, against his old club Arsenal.

Brian Hornsby played 120 times for Sheffield Wednesday and showed a goal return of 30, a very health ratio for any midfielder. Although, not quite as high as we all thought it may be, after his stunning 24 goals in his first 60 games. Brian moved on to Chesterfield and later the USA.

Brian Hornsby (Sheffield Wednesday)

John Hickton was sold by Alan Brown to Middlesbrough four months after the 1966 cup final defeat by Everton. He was a player who was never given a real run in the side. He played for two seasons at Hillsborough, managing 26 games in season 1964-65 and 24 games in 1965-66. He scored 10 and 11 goals respectively.

50 games and 21 goals, a good ratio for any striker and it has to be pointed out that Hickton was played at full back and centre half in some of those games. It must have crossed Hickton's mind that a place in the Cup Final line up was also up for grabs when centre back Vic Mobley was injured in the cup semi final, Mr Brown overlooked him selecting an inexperienced Sam Ellis.

Derek Dooley, who looked after the juniors, was a big believer in Hickton's scoring ability and he was proved correct, when at his new club, Middlesbrough, John proceeded to score over 80 goals in his first 150 games. He went on to score 192 goals for the Ayresome park club in just over 400 games.

John Hickton (Sheffield Wednesday)

Niclas Alexandersson who signed for Wednesday from his home town club of Halmstad only stayed with the Owls for a couple of seasons. He was, an attack minded, right sided player who offered Wednesday the benefit of being able to play midfield and also play as an out and out right winger. He was never a prolific scorer but did knock in a few telling goals for the Owls. He always seemed to be on the scoresheet for his national side, Sweden. He scored the equaliser against England in the the Japan-Korean World Cup finals of 2002.

Niclas Alexandersson (Sheff Wed & Sweden)

Niclas was an intelligent player who came into the side as Wednesday seemed to be sliding towards relegation, he put his all into saving the team from the drop and he was never one to shirk his responsibility on the pitch. When the Owls were relegated he could have gone to a few clubs but decided, it seemed, rather unwisely on Everton FC.

Paul Williams was born on16th August, 1965 in London, 25 years and 11 days later he made his debut for Sheffield Wednesday in what was to be the best season the supporters at Hillsborough had seen for decades. Paul only played 111 games in total for the Owls but he was such an important part of the team in season 1990-91. His tally of 17 goals helped Wednesday to gain promotion and win the League Cup. He was also instrumental in a large number of the goals his striking partner, David Hirst, scored.

Paul was only a slight built young man, 5ft 7inches, but he was lightning fast and was never afraid to go in where he knew it would hurt.

The following season, under new manager, Trevor Francis, he played fewer games only making 31 starting appearances but still managing a respectable 10 goals.

In his third season he only managed one goal in 7 appearances and Trevor Francis let him move away from Sheffield.

Paul Williams (Sheffield Wednesday)

Lawrie Madden was offered terms at Arsenal in the late 70s but turned it down to concentrate on his academic studies, in Economics and Social Studies, at Manchester University. After gaining his degree he joined Charlton Athletic and played in 113 games before being transferred to Millwall in March 1982. After 47 apperances at the Den, Sheffield Wednesday stepped in and brought him to Hillsborough in August 1983.

Madden played over 240 games for the Owls and was at Hillsborough through the good times. He arrived just as Wednesday were gaining promotion from the second division and played a vital part in keeping a steady sound defence. Lawrie, who averaged around 30 games a season in his 8 years at Hillsborough, was a reliable organiser of the back line and his understanding of positional play made him a very valuable player.

He came on as substitute in the Wembley Cup Final of 1991 to gain a well deserved winners medal in one of his last games for the Owls.

Lawrie Madden (Sheffield Wednesday)

The **Managers**

Sheffield Wednesday, technically did not have a manager from the creation of the club in 1867 up until 1920. For the latter part of this time a chap named Arthur Dickinson was the secretary of the club and worked alongside the board and made team selection. This situation would be ludicrous now, but to give the club credit, during this time Wednesday won both the League Championship and FA Cup twice. The Championship winning years were 1902-03, 1903-04, and the FA Cup winning years were 1896 and 1907.

From 1920 until 1933, Bob Brown managed the Owls and won two more League Championships in 1928-1929 and 1929-30.

From 1933 until 1937 Billy Walker was in charge of the Owls and led Wednesday to their last FA Cup final victory, 4-2 against West Bromwich Albion. Wednesday went on to win the FA Charity Shield against Arsenal before the start of the next season.

Jimmy McMullan came into the manager's job in 1937 and stayed until 1942 when his contract was not renewed. This was to be a thankless task for McMullan because within 18 months of being placed in charge at Hillsborough, Europe was in the early throes of the Second World War and games could not be planned with any certainty and leagues had to be condensed to suit local areas. With average gates of around 25,000 in season 1938-39 the following few seasons were a difficult period in Sheffield Wednesday's history as well as Britain's. The average crowd for games in the first three years of the war were 4,000. McMullan was possibly dismissed for the simple reason Wednesday could not afford his salary.

It is amazing though that people managed to carry on through what was the blitz period for Sheffield and still keep attending games, albeit in much smaller numbers.

Possibly to save money, Eric Taylor was named the new manager of Sheffield Wednesday in 1942. He started at Hillsborough as office boy to Bob Brown in 1929. In his first season in charge he managed to get Wednesday to the North War Cup Final, which sadly they lost over two legs to Blackpool. At the end of the war in 1945, Taylor was confirmed as secretary-manager. It was under Taylor that Sheffield Wednesday gained the title of the Yo-Yo team, with promotion in 1950, relegation in 1951, 1954 and 1958 and gaining Second Division titles in 1952 and 1956. In fact it was the relegation in 1958 that prompted Taylor to relinquish the team manager duties and look for a new manager.

Harry Catterick was the new manager who started in August 1958 and within that season had turned almost the same bunch of relegated players into Champions of Division Two. In the three years he was at Hillsborough he set the foundation for some of the best years of my time watching Sheffield Wednesday. Catterick went back to his former club Everton in1961.

Vic Buckingham was to follow and he did nothing at all wrong, in my humble opinion, but sixth place in all his three seasons was deemed a failure.

Alan Brown was next on the list, a man who moulded Brian Clough into what he was - enough said. He was a strict disciplinarian, who in his four years managed positions of 8th, 11th, 17th and 19th in Division One.

At this point, February 1968, I think a revolving door was placed on the manager's office - Jack Marshall, Danny Williams, Derek Dooley, Steve Burtenshaw, Len Ashurst, Jack Charlton, Howard Wilkinson, Peter Eustace, Ron Atkinson, Trevor Francis, David Pleat, Danny Wilson, Paul Jewell, Peter Shreeves, Terry Yorath, Chris Turner and, as I write, Paul Sturrock.

In this 37 year span, only Jack Charlton and Howard Wilkinson have managed Wednesday for longer than four years.

Sheffield

Harry **Catterick**

Harry Catterick was the manager of Sheffield Wednesday for only 33 months, between August 1958 and April 1961, but what a glorious time that was to be an Owls supporter.

Catterick was born in the Darlington area and played in the centre forward position for Everton for 14 seasons. Unfortunately for him he played in the shadow of the legendary Tommy Lawton and Jock Dodds, therefore only managing 71 first team appearances.

He left Everton to take the player manager's position at Crewe where he stayed for two years before moving to Rochdale where he had five good seasons.

It was at this point in his career that Sheffield Wednesday stepped in and appointed him manager in 1958. In his first season in charge he sold the golden boy of Sheffield soccer, Albert Quixall, and replaced him with an almost unknown, Johnny Fantham, and developed youngsters like Kay, Swan, and Springett into players who blossomed into footballers who eventually would represent their country.

The team he took on to promotion in season 1958-59 was basically the team that had finished in last place (22nd) in the First Division, with the exception of Quixall.

In season 1959-60 he brought Megson in to the starting line up and bought a wee little midfield player called Bobby Craig, for a fee of £6,500 from Third Lanark. This was the maximum fee paid out by Catterick in his three years at Hillsborough, even though he did pocket £45,000 for Quixall from Manchester United, a British record at the time. With these alterations in the team structure a real quality side started to develop. He had options up front with the old guard Froggatt playing 18 games and notching up half a dozen goals. Fantham who was now starting to gain confidence knocking in 18 goals. Keith Ellis, a young man who had been at the club for six years with only a handful of games, now given a chance, scored 13 times in 22 appearances. And with wingers Finney and Wilkinson both getting into double figures it was a solid return to the top flight in English football where a very respectable fifth place was achieved.

Along with the fine league position we reached the FA Cup semi-final against Blackburn, sadly losing 2-1. On the way to the semi, Wednesday defeated Manchester United at Old Trafford and Sheffield United in the quarter final at Bramall Lane.

Catterick's third season in charge was filled with expectation. Players such as Swan and Springett had gained full England caps, Megson, Fantham and Kay all played for the English league and with this nucleus of talent it seemed we could take anybody on, home or away. The season started stunningly 12 games into the season before we had a setback, losing to Wolves. In the 15th game of the season the real crunch game against Tottenham Hotspur was played at Hillsborough. Spurs who had not been defeated all season and were looking good for the Championship, even at that early stage of the season, arrived at Hillsborough on November 12th. The crowd that night was 56,363, the largest crowd I have been in at Hillsborough. Wednesday won 2-1, with goals from Griffin and Fantham. At this point we were ecstatic and could see the championship on the horizon. Sadly we proceeded to lose the next three league games, and second place in the First Division was the best we could achieve. Spurs who eventually won the league also lifted the FA Cup, the first side to do so in the 20th century. That second position in the league was Wednesday's best effort in over 30 years and it is still better than we have achieved since.

Catterick was a hero and with him at the helm we could actually win some silverware. Sadly, at the end of the 1960-61 season, Harry moved back to his old club Everton, possibly lured by a club with much looser purse strings. It has been said Catterick would have been happy to stay at Hillsborough given a little more buying power and a little less dominance from Eric Taylor.

Catterick was a manager destined to be a winner and with Everton he proved this with league titles and FA cup wins. He also knew a good player, making a quick swoop back to Hillsborough to purchase his old Tony Kay, for a then British record fee for a wing half of £55,000.

Vic **Buckingham**

I remember Vic Buckingham coming to Sheffield Wednesday in May 1961. Even as a 12 years old, I thought he would have to be a good manager to follow in the footsteps of Harry Catterick who gained such lofty positions for the Owls with so little cash resources.

To give Buckingham his due, he was a good manager, and he had proved this elsewhere.

After his football career ended, he played full back for 15 seasons at Tottenham Hotspur (1935-1950), he guided Pegasus to an FA Amateur Cup win in 1951 and West Bromwich Albion to an FA Cup victory in 1954. He followed this by being one of the first English managers to be offered a coaching position abroad, this was in Holland where he guided Ajax of Amsterdam to the Dutch League Championship and to National Cup success. He was also the man who discovered Johann Cruyff. So Vic Buckingham came to Sheffield Wednesday with a strong managerial reputation.

His first season in charge was 1961-1962 and expectations were high after achieving second place in the top division the season before. With the same group of players that Catterick had used plus Colin Dobson and Edwin Holliday, (bought from Middlesborough) Wednesday, unfortunately, did not match the previous league results. At Hillsborough their form was almost as good as the season before but away from home the results were poor, only six wins out of 21 games. So in Buckingham's first season Sheffield Wednesday managed sixth place. They had qualified for the Fairs Cup and played Olympique Lyonnais in the first round beating them 7-6 on aggregate. Roma were next and a good aggregate win of 4-1 with a Gerry Young hat-trick in the home game secured Wednesday's place in the quarter finals. Here we played one of the big boys of European football, Barcelona. Sheffield Wednesday won the home leg 3-2 with Fantham 2 and Finney the scorers. Unfortunately the Spanish team won the return leg 2-0 and sadly, the Owls' first journey into European competition was ended.

Buckingham's second season was almost in contrast to his first 12 months, Wednesday's home form got worse, only 10 wins, but we picked up as many points on our travels as when we finished second. Vic also made one of the best transfer

deals any Wednesday manager has done in my 50 years of visiting Hillsborough. He signed David Layne. Layne went straight into the team at the start of season 1962-63, and in his first 13 games he had netted 12 times. He finished the season with 30 goals from his 42 appearances, four of them against Sheffield United.

It was also in this season that Wednesday pulled off a coup with the arranging of a friendly with Pele's club side, Santos. Over 49,000 of us turned up to watch Santos run out 4-2 winners. Pele, twice a world cup winner and still only 23 years old, scored from the penalty spot.

At the end of Buckingham's second season he achieved 6th place in the First Division, again.

Season 1963-64, Buckingham's third season, and as usual there were high expectations from the supporters. The Owls were back to fortress Hillsborough with 15 wins, but the away form, again, was very poor, only four wins. Wednesday had qualified for the European Fairs Cup and demolished DOS Utrecht 8-2 on aggregate in the first round. The second round threw up stronger opposition, FC Cologne, and the Owls lost 5-3 after both legs. David Layne managed 5 goals in the four games.

At the season's end Vic Buckingham had managed for three terms and finished in sixth position in all of them. He had seen the Owls play in European club football for the first time and regained entry into the same competition in his third season. He purchased David Layne, a real gem, and he played Gerry Young at wing half, where he later won England honours. He introduced young players like Colin Dobson, Peter Eustace, Vic Mobley and David Ford. He gained, albeit slightly, more points in every one of his three seasons. This was not deemed good enough by the powers that be at Hillsborough and Buckingham's contract was not renewed at the end of season 1963-64.

It took Sheffield Wednesday well over 20 years to reach a position as high as sixth again in the first division, and it has only been bettered twice in over 40 years.

Oh, for the days of sixth position in three consecutive seasons in the top flight.

Wednesday

Jack **Charlton**

October 1977 was a good year for Sheffield Wednesday. We didn't know it at the time but the arrival of Jack Charlton was to be the start of a move back to where we belong, the top division. Taking over from Len Ashurst part way through the 1977-1978 season he could only manage 14th place in Division Three in his first season. To be honest his next season was no better, finishing in the same position, but he was bringing in new players and introducing some young local born lads to make the side a team to get out of the dreaded Third Division. He bought Curran, a revelation in his first season, Brian Hornsby a class act who notched 21 goals from midfield in season 1978-79, and Mike Lyons, whose experience steadied the defence. He also signed Gary Megson and made a stunning transfer buy in Gary Shelton. Gary Bannister was a striker who scored 22 goals in every one of his three seasons at Hillsborough. He chose Bolder in goal at the expense of Turner, making it a sounder defence. He started Peter Shirtliff, Mark Smith and Mel Sterland on all three of their illustrious careers.

I think it could be said Jack's only transfer failure was the Yugoslav, Ante Mirocevic who played 48 games and scored only three goals.

Jack came out of retirement to manage Sheffield Wednesday. He had been in charge at Middlesborough whom he guided in to the First Division in his first season and then decided he needed to have some quality time off. His hobbies of fishing and shooting took up his daylight hours and he earned a lucrative living after dinner speaking as well as being a voiciferous TV soccer pundit. He did put his foot in it a few times but it was always from the heart and when he said he would have chinned a certain player it was his genuine off the cuff response and he was all the more liked for it.

After two years of mid table finishes Charlton took Wednesday to promotion to Division Two in 1980 and you literally felt the buzz come back into Hillsborough.

The next three seasons were more of the same, getting that little bit better all the time, with 10th, 6th and 4th placings in the second division and playing some good football, just missing out on promotion by one point in season 1982. Not enough credit goes to Charlton for the high level of football his teams played. In 1983 he took Sheffield Wednesday to the FA Cup semi finals against Brighton, once again we lost at this stage 2-1 with Mirocevic scoring the Owls goal.

Then five and a half years after he came (he promised to stay for five) he decided it was time to move on. The one thing you could guarantee: if Jack had made his mind up it was no use trying to change it.

A couple of years later he was to take on the manager's position of Ireland (Eire) and he guided them through the qualification sections to the final stages of two World Cups. He was once again the hero, even to the Irish who didn't really want to have an Englishman as head of their national squad.

What Charlton did with most of these teams was to sort out the defence first and get discipline into the back line. Get a real experienced defender in there to sort it out and cut out the mistakes. You are more than half way to a good side if you don't leak goals.

Jack Charlton was a Godsend to Sheffield Wednesday coming 11 years and six managers after the 1966 cup final defeat and stopped a downward slide that had set in after Everton had beaten us at Wembley.

Jackie Charlton started his football life with Leeds United and remained there all of his playing career, appearing in over 600 games. He won the League Championship, FA Cup, League Cup, Fairs Cup, and to top all of those he is one of only eleven Englishmen to win a World Cup Winners Medal in 1966.

He was only the European Championship winners medal short of a full house of medals possible for an English player . His brother Bobby did win that one, so it was within the family trophy cabinet.

Sheffield

Howard **Wilkinson**

When Jack Charlton resigned, the man selected to fill his position was the manager of Notts County, Howard Wilkinson, who when offered the position jumped at the chance to manage his old club.

Howard arrived in the June of 1983, a couple of months before the new season. He started with 'old Jack's' team except for three players. The goalkeeper, Bolder was replaced by Martin Hodge. Up front McCulloch's position was taken by Imre Varadi and a defender, Lawrie Madden, was brought in. The defence shipped 13 less goals and Varadi scored 19 goals, nine more than McCulloch. With his understanding of what was needed to get out of the second division it looked like we were on to a winner with old Howard. Halfway through his first season Howard purchased two more players: Tony Cunningham and Nigel Worthington. The former did not work out but the latter was to stay at Hillsborough for over ten years, playing over 400 games, and only moved when Howard, then Leeds manager, came for him in 1994.

It went so well for Howard and Wednesday in that first season, it was our 16th game before a loss, a 1-0 defeat at Crystal Palace. We only lost another four games all season and gained a points haul of 88 to finish in second place and win promotion back to the top division. It was 14 years since that awful, depressing, rainsoaked night against Manchester City on April 22nd 1970. We were back where we belonged.

Wilkinson had one major close season problem, he had to deal with the fact that Gary Bannister, the fan's hero, wanted to leave. He was subsequently transferred to QPR. This left a big gap to fill, 20 plus goals in all his three seasons was good going at any level. Howard dealt with the situation with his usual aplomb and bought Lee Chapman. I have to say, I did not think this was the correct decision and a lumbering lad like Chapman would not get the same amount of goals as Bannister did. Chapman did get the amount Bannister did and in a higher division as well, so that is why Howard Wilkinson is a football manager and I am just a fan.

Howard was never out of his depth in the First Division and proved this with finishing positions of 8th and 5th in his first two seasons. The crowds had come back, the team was playing good stuff and we were gaining victories at places like Anfield, Old Trafford, even doing a double double over the mighty Manchester United in our first two seasons back in the top division. Also in our second season, 1985-86, we once again reached a semi-final of the FA cup, against Everton at Villa Park which Wednesday lost 2-1 with Carl Shutt scoring the Owls goal.

The third season in Division One was a little bit of an anti-climax, only managing 13th position. I think this could possibly be put down to the fact that around the turn of the year we lost the services of our two central defenders, Hart and Knight. Paul Hart was surprisingly allowed to join Birmingham City, where on his debut he broke his leg, and young Ian Knight had his leg badly broken by a horrendous tackle by Bennett of Chester City and never recovered enough to play top class football again. Larry May was purchased to fill one of the gaps left in defence, he proved to be a disappointing purchase. The defensive problem was not really solved until October 1987 when Nigel Pearson arrived from Shrewsbury. Howard's other notable purchase that season was a young man called David Hirst.

In Howard's last full season, mid table was again achieved, but we were not heading in the right direction. Some of the players decided that leaving Hillsborough would be good for them as the club seemed to be purchasing cheap cast off players – Tony Galvin, Colin West, Ian Cranston and Steve McCall, rather than going for quality. Wilkinson had agreed fees for Mark Wright and Chris Fairclough but Wednesday could not match the demands of the players. I think Wilkinson saw this as lack of ambition by the Wednesday board and when offered the Leeds post, in October 1988, he accepted.

I think, Howard Wilkinson is the only ex-Sheffield Wednesday player to manage the Owls who decided to leave as opposed to being sacked.

Ron **Atkinson**

Ron Atkinson started his football career at Aston Villa. He didn't make the grade and was released on a free transfer to Headington United, soon to become Oxford United. Atkinson captained them to two southern league titles and in 1962 they gained admitance to the football league. Within six years Oxford United had gained two promotions and were in division two. Ron played over 550 games for Oxford United in a 15 year stay.

He left to take up a managerial position at Kettering Town, where he stayed for three years before a league club, Cambridge United, sought out his managerial skills. He did not disappoint and in his first season he gained them promotion as champions of division four. From that point onwards he was hot property in the football world and a few clubs were chasing his signature to be their new boss. He chose West Bromwich Albion in January 1978. In his three seasons at the Hawthornes he gained a third and a fourth place in the top division and reached an FA Cup semi final.

Ron was an ambitious type and when Manchester United came calling he didn't think too hard or too long about taking the job. In his five years at Manchester he won two FA Cup finals, a Charity Shield and never finished outside of the top four places. To the Red Devils that is almost failure and Ron was axed in 1986, albeit with a tasty compensation package.

In February 1989 after Sheffield Wednesday had sacked Peter Eustace, Ron Atkinson, for the third time, was asked to take over as manager of the Owls. He accepted.

Atkinson was first asked to manage at Hillsborough in the mid 70s when they were in the third division, he declined. His second refusal was just after Wilkinson left Hillsborough. So it was third time lucky for Sheffield Wednesday.

Ron came in, initially, to save Wednesday from relegation. The team, under the guidance of Peter Eustace, had been on a disasterous run. Atkinson came in with 15 games left, the team gained 19 points from these games and just staved off the drop. Things now looked bright for the Owls fans and the new season could not come quick enough. We had a high profile manager at last and that would help us get some of the players who possibly would not come for the lesser managers in the game. In his first few months at the club he showed a profit on transfer deals, Palmer, Whitton and Bennett came in and West, Proctor and Sterland went out.

Alas, it was around this time that the most tragic disaster in British football happened on the Leppings Lane end of Hillsborough. The semi-final, 15th April 1989, between Notts Forest and Liverpool saw the death of 95 Liverpool supporters who were crushed to death as the surge from behind pressed the poor souls at the front into the fencing at pitchside. The final and 96th victim of the Hillsborough disaster, Tony Bland, died in 1993, after spending four years in a coma.

The Leppings Lane terracing stayed closed for a considerable period and did not help with the atmosphere within Hillsborough. The next season was a vast anti-climax and Wedneday were relegated in 1990. Even with this disasterous outcome Ron Atkinson was still buying quality players who would lead Wednesday into their best period for decades. He purchased Roland Nilsson who chose the Owls over Manchester United, John Sheridan, Phil King, Danny Wilson, Paul Williams, Dalian Atkinson, John Harkes and Trevor Francis.

Season 1990-1991 was a good year to be an Owls fan. We gained promotion back to the top flight, and gained the only major success in my 50 years of watching the Owls, the League Cup. It was made all the sweeter because we beat Manchester United. Sweet for the fans but I imagine for Atkinson even more so.

After the League Cup final, Wednesday still had to clinch promotion, so no celebrations were planned just yet. Ron wanted the civic reception to be held when the return to the top division was in the bag. This the Owls proceeded to achieve.

Just before the planned civic reception, to celebrate the Owls' double achievement, Aston Villa came in with an offer for Atkinson. It was, he says, too good to turn down. He did still live in the Midlands and he probably saw a little more cash and potential at Villa Park – who knows.

This caused some of the supporters to label him a Judas, but to be fair to Big Ron his 27 month stay did leave Wednesday in a lot better shape than he found us in. We had quality players in every position and he also set up our next manager, Trevor Francis, with whom we had some memorable times. Ron Atkinson is the only post war Owls manager to win a trophy, other than lower divisional titles.

I grew up in Attercliffe in the late forties and early fifties where I lived with my grandfather. He set his stall out to bring my up as an Owl. He knew my father was a Unitedite, so it was his duty to teach me the true path, which he did with stories about Robinson, Starling, Blenkinsop, Hooper, Rimmer, Millership and others. These were some of the players he saw, who had won every honour in the game. I loved the blue and white stripes of Wednesday before I ever saw the team play.

My grandfather regaled me with all the stories, but the actual task of taking me on the bus to the city centre and then the football special to Hillsborough fell on the shoulders of my father. He did not mind, because he always went to see which ever Sheffield club was playing at home.

I cannot say I remember my early visits with much clarity. It was about three years later, about the time of Ron Springett's arrival in 1958, that all the names and faces seemed to click in to the memory banks. In my school holidays I would walk to Hillsborough with a couple of friends, Lee Froggatt and Allan Dent, to collect the players' autographs, and watch them train. Then there would be the spending of my dinner money on bubble gum cards instead of stopping for dinner. You could buy twelve of these cards for the price of a school dinner. It was never a contest, although, being hungry, I never left any of the meals my mother cooked for me in the evenings. I collected all the programmes from my Hillsborough visits, bubble gum cards, autographs, basically anything I could lay my hands on that was connected to Sheffield Wednesday FC. I recall when the Charles Buchan Football Monthly had a colour picture of a Wednesday player, I was ecstatic and, for some reason, used to buy two copies. I had scrapbooks full of newspaper cuttings and magazine articles as well as my spare autographs.

I must have had about 30 signatures from Ron Springett. He must have thought I was a juvenile stalker.

Like most supporters I have my favourite era, and to me it will always be the five years from Harry Catterick gaining us promotion to the end of Vic Buckingham's Hillsborough career. The team, which included great players like Ron Springett, Peter Swan, Redfern Froggatt, Tony Kay, Alan Finney, Don Megson, Johhny Fantham, David Layne, Colin Dobson, Gerry Young and Peter Johnson, never finished outside of the top six in Division One in all of those five seasons.

Gary Mackender, the artist who drew the players in this book, is a little younger than myself and his favourite era is the late 80s and early 90s. To be fair, this was a good period in Wednesday's history, with players like, Chris Waddle, Roland Nilsson, Nigel Pearson, David Hirst, John Sheridan, Carlton Palmer and Des Walker.

Would the team from the Cup winning era have beaten that sixties side? Gary and myself have differing opinions on that one.

Gary has, wonderfully, illustrated some of the Sheffield Wednesday players through a 65 year time span, from Ronnie Starling (c 1935) through to Paulo to Di Canio (c 2000). He has also captured some of the many strips that Sheffield Wednesday have worn over the years.

Abby Currier has illustrated the managers and even though she had never heard of some of them made an excellent job of capturing the men who were at the helm of the club when the good times were at Hillsborough.

Ackowledgements

I would like to thank **Sheffield Wednesday Football Club**, and particularly **Steve Chu** Communications Manager at Hillsborough, for his assistance;

Eric Brodie (author of *The Jackie Robinson Story*) for his invaluable and generous help with some of the autographs and pictures of the Sheffield Wednesday players;

Linda Mackender for decorating the house whilst her husband, Gary, sat around drawing the pictures for the book!